how to grow
African
Violets

By the Editors of *Sunset Books* and *Sunset Magazine*

LANE BOOKS • MENLO PARK, CALIFORNIA

Foreword

The intensive cultivation of African violets really began in this century, so that most knowledge about them and the multitude of excellent hybrids are of recent origin. That so much has been done in a relatively short time is a testimony to the attraction these flowers possess.

Work on this book was made easier by the selfless cooperation of various dedicated African violet growers who have long been captured by this attraction. We would like to give thanks to Buell's Greenhouses, Eastford, Connecticut; Fischer Greenhouses, Linwood, New Jersey; Lyndon Lyon, Dolgeville, New York; Betty Stoehr, Greenwood, Indiana; Sunnyside Nurseries, Hayward, California; Tinari Greenhouses, Huntingdon Valley, Pennsylvania; and Alma Wright, Knoxville, Tennessee. Also of invaluable aid were the African Violet Society of America and its publication, *The African Violet Magazine*; and the American Gesneria Society and the Saintpaulia International and their bimonthly journal, *Gesneriad-Saintpaulia News*. Lists of African violet hybrids on pages 64–79 were compiled from listings which appeared in *The African Violet Magazine* and in *Gesneriad-Saintpaulia News*. This is by no means a complete roster of African violets, but it represents a selection of some of the fine hybrids sold today.

Researched and written by Jack Kramer

Edited by Philip Edinger

Design: Lawrence A. Laukhuf

Illustrations: Steve Holland

Front cover: Rhapsodie 'Gisela'; photograph by Joyce R. Wilson
Back cover: Rhapsodie 'Gigi', photograph by George Selland, Moss photography; all other photographs courtesy of Fischer Greenhouses, Linwood, New Jersey

Third Printing June 1972

Contents

SIMPLE BUT ELEGANT table decoration is possible with a single, well-grown African violet plant and selected accessories. This plant's pot is inserted into hammered copper bowl.

The Natural Beauty of African Violets

Have you been searching for a house plant which will give you flowers throughout the year, that will not outgrow its bounds, and that will grow happily in the same temperature and humidity ranges that you, too, prefer? Then you ought to consider growing African violets. Not only do they satisfy the foregoing requirements, but they also are available in great variety of colors, foliage types, and styles of flowers so that there is always something new to keep your interest and enthusiasm going. Furthermore, they can be used indoors in many ways (see Chapter 3), including—in addition to the traditional plant displays at windows—groupings under fluorescent lights in any part of any room. Along with all these advantages, they are inexpensive—and so easy to propagate that in no time at all you can grow enough new plants to more than satisfy your own needs and those of your friends as well.

FROM AFRICA TO POPULARITY

The resemblance of their flowers to those of true violets is partially responsible for the popular name "African violets" by which these plants are known; the "African" part of the name does, indeed, reflect the continent of their origin. Botanically these plants are called *Saintpaulia*; the most important species are described on pages 9–10. In the larger sense, African violets (Saintpaulias) belong to the family Gesneriaceae which includes a number of other popular house plants (such as the florists' gloxinias) which you will meet in the chapter beginning on page 42.

In two separate locations in northeast Tanganyika, African violets were discovered and collected by a German colonial official and planter—the Baron Walter von Saint Paul—in 1892. Records are unclear as to whether he sent plants or seeds to his father in northern Germany, but in either case plants flowered there in 1893—for the first time outside of their native Africa.

Upon seeing these plants in flower, the director of the Royal Botanic Garden at Herrenhausen realized that they were a new find in the plant world and named the genus *Saintpaulia* in honor of the father and son who discovered and grew them. The species then flowering he named *ionantha*, which means "with violet-like flowers." Within only a few years after its introduction to

'NORSEMAN' is one of the original ten hybrids from Armacost & Royston. The very blue flowers are carried profusely above velvety foliage.

horticultural circles, the African violet was being grown and offered for sale by several European seed and plant firms.

During this period (still before 1900) a sharp-eyed grower noticed that some of the plants produced seed capsules that were long and slender while others had rounded capsules. Not until well into this century was it realized that the Baron von Saint Paul had sent *two* species to his father. Those with rounded capsules are now recognized as *Saintpaulia ionantha*, while the long-fruited species was appropriately designated S. *confusa*.

The Age of Development

Although African violet plants had been introduced to this country shortly after their discovery, they made no particular impact among greenhouse and houseplant fanciers. Very likely this was because the early growers in America knew so little of how to care for these exotics that the plants gave up in despair. However, in 1927 the Los Angeles nursery firm of Armacost & Royston, Inc. imported African violet seeds from an English

seed house and from the one in Germany which 30 years earlier had noticed the seed capsule differences. Something in the neighborhood of 1,000 plants were grown from these seeds; selections from these seedlings launched the African violet popularity wave that to this day is still growing.

Originally there were ten selections from the Armacost and Royston plants. Of the German seedlings, two were given names: 'Blue Boy' and 'Sailor Boy.' 'Admiral,' 'Amethyst,' 'Commodore,' 'Mermaid,' 'Neptune,' 'Norseman,' 'No. 32,' and 'Viking' came from the English seed. All were in the violet-purple-blue color range. Although newer originations show considerable variation from these originals, some of these first ten hybrids still compare favorably with others in their color classes. Some African violet shows have special categories for exhibiting these first hybrids.

The African violet we know today is a product of intensive hybridization, but most of this involves only the two species which were once thought to be one—and that were in the background of the Armacost & Royston hybrids. The first differences in flower and foliage forms arose

AFRICAN VIOLET TERMINOLOGY

The considerable variation you find in African violet flowers and foliage—both in color and shapes—has brought forth a list of descriptive terms particular to these plants. Some of these terms are self-explanatory; those that aren't were coined from the name of the variety that first exhibited the characteristic.

The photograph below shows many but not all of the possible foliage and flower variations. The first descriptions refer to the photograph (background grid is 1-inch squares).

1. Plain leaf, sometimes called "boy" foliage after the variety 'Blue Boy.'
2. "Girl" leaf, named for the hybrid 'Blue Girl' which was a mutation from 'Blue Boy'; distinguishing feature is the white spot at the leaf base.
3. Oak leaf, with slightly indented margins.
4. Quilted leaf, with distinctly raised areas between leaf veins.
5. Fluted leaf.
6. Serrated leaf edge.
7. Variegated leaf—green and cream-white.
8. Black-green leaf.
9. A heavily rippled leaf, almost bordering on fringe.
10. Holly-type foliage.
A. Plain, single flower typical of the species and most of the early hybrids.

B. Semi-double flower has a few extra petaloids but stamens are clearly visible.
C. Single "star" flower, easy to recognize because of the five equally spaced and sized petals.
D. Double flower has additional full-sized petals.
E. Single fringed flower. Petal edges are comparable to the leaf edge of number 9.
F. Bicolor double flower—petals and edges are two different colors.
G. Fringed double flower.
H. Crested double flower, where extra petals obscure the stamens by forming a crest-like projection.
I. Fantasy flower with irregular dashes of color on the petals.

Here are some additional terms you may encounter.

Geneva: flowers have white petal edges (the first hybrid to show this was 'Lady Geneva').
Longifolia: leaf is long, narrow, and pointed.
Spoon: leaf has rolled-up margin, particularly toward the stem end.
Strawberry: foliage is puckered and serrated like a strawberry leaf.
Supreme: a plant which has large, heavy-textured and brittle foliage and flowers. These arose as mutations from other hybrids (such as 'Blue Boy Supreme').

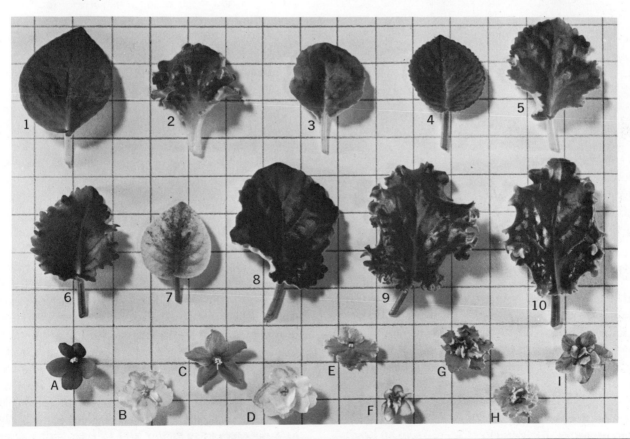

DU PONT HYBRID (top) has larger leaves, flowers than conventional hybrid (below).

as mutations from named varieties (see page 7). Subsequent crosses of these with other named varieties established these mutant characteristics (doubleness, for example) and afforded new combinations of foliage, color, and form. The Fringette series, which came from the Fischer Greenhouses years ago, were the first flowers to have frilled and ruffled petals. The Fantasy line has blossoms of one color streaked or splotched with another. The duPont strain has thick, hairy, quilted leaves and very large flowers (although less of them). The newer Rhapsodie series is noted for its abundant growth and bloom.

The variations continue to go on and on so that now there is an almost infinite variety of flower form and coloring and in leaf texture. Some blossoms resemble buttercups, others are star-shaped. There are varieties with flowers of snowy white, all shades of pink, crimson red, wine and purple-red, and all conceivable variations and intensities in the original blue and purple colors. Departing from the solid colors, you can find flowers that are delicately edged with red, blue, or white (or even green!); others may be irregularly splashed with color; still others may have darker centers that fade out to the petal edges or may have upper petal lobes darker than the lower ones. And to compound the possibilities, all these color arrangements may appear (depending upon the particular variety) in flowers that are single, semi-double, or fully double.

In addition to concentrating on improving flower colors and color combinations, hybridizers have been busy developing different growth habits. While there always have been certain varieties that would, with good care, make plants considerably larger than others in a collection, the production of definitely miniature varieties establishes the greatest size difference. These plants, and the somewhat larger semi-miniatures, are perfect scaled-down replicas of full-sized African violets—available in just about the same variety of colors, and great space savers where growing room is limited. Fewer in number than the miniature varieties but just as distinct a departure in plant habit are the hybrids which will trail over the edges of pots instead of forming compact rosettes. Most of these hybrids probably stem from the species *S. grotei* which is a naturally trailing sort.

THE WILD ONES

The African violet species—all native to hills and mountains of East Africa—may at first seem somewhat unexciting if you compare them to some of the ruffled, fringed, double, and multicolored hybrids. But if you look at them alongside hybrids to which they are more directly comparable (i.e. single blue or violet flowers) you may be surprised by how good some of them look for plants that have not been "improved" by man. At the very least you will find them interesting, and part of this interest stems from the knowledge that presumably just two species (S. *ionantha* and S. *confusa*) are in the ancestry of nearly all modern hybrids and are responsible for the almost incredible divergence from wild flower and foliage types. It's hard not to wonder what new characteristics might lie hidden in the other species, awaiting only some enterprising hybridizers to bring them to light.

Here are brief descriptions of each of the most important species now recognized.

Saintpaulia amaniensis is one of the few species having creeping stems; these will cascade over the edge of a pot or will root where they come into contact with the soil if given the chance. Flowers are light blue-violet with darker centers; rounded leaves are medium green with almost white reverses. Closer investigation has deprived this plant of its specific status and classified it as a variation of S. *magungensis*, but in many books you will find it listed as a separate species. It needs more water, less light, and lower temperatures than most named hybrids.

S. *confusa* bears clusters of deep violet flowers above medium to light green leaves that are smooth, flat, and slightly quilted. It shows off best when allowed to develop multiple crowns; otherwise it is a small plant that will tend to grow at an angle toward the side of its pot.

S. *difficilis* is easily grown as a single-crown plant; the leaves are definitely veined, long-pointed, often spooned, and carried at the ends of long, upright-growing leaf stalks. Flowers are medium to deep blue.

S. *diplotricha* forms small single-crowned rosettes of deep green to purplish green thick leaves, paler on their undersides. Flowers are a very pale blue-lilac that approaches white.

S. *goetziana* is reputed difficult to grow, requiring cool temperature, high humidity, and subdued light. This is another trailing species which sends up numerous rosettes of small dark leaves from a creeping stem, so that the general effect is pincushion-like. Flowers are such a pale lavender that they are nearly white.

S. *grandifolia* grows as a rather large single-crowned plant—the long leaf-stalks angle upward and carry thin-textured, oval, medium green leaves. The large clusters of violet flowers are very showy.

S. *grotei* is the best known of the trailing species, the stems of which may reach lengths of 3 feet on well-grown plants. Flat, medium-green leaves are borne on the ends of distinctive brown leaf-stalks. Flowers are blue-violet with darker centers. Give plants shade and much moisture but perfect drainage.

S. *intermedia* grows either as a single- or multiple-crowned plant with an upright habit. The nearly round olive green leaves have a tendency

'GIRL' FOLIAGE *is shown by white spot at base of leaves. This is first of the type: 'Blue Girl.'*

FAMOUS ANCESTOR of nearly all named hybrids is Saintpaulia ionantha *with variable blue blossoms. This species also is pictured on page 42.*

to spoon. It produces its blue flowers with no special care.

S. ionantha, like *S. confusa,* appears to be in the background of modern hybrids. It bears blue-violet flowers, and the leaves are dark green, quilted, and with serrated edges. Growth is single-crowned and upright.

S. magungensis is another trailing species. It has small, rounded to heart-shaped leaves which tend to cup under slightly and are much paler on their undersides. Flowers are a medium blue-violet shading to darker centers.

S. nitida is a small species with shiny dark leaves and dark violet-blue flowers. The leaf-stalks are slender, flexible, and brown to purplish green.

S. orbicularis grows best as a multiple-crowned plant. The rounded shiny dark green leaves with their purplish-brown leaf stalks contrast nicely with the small light lilac, dark-centered blooms. In its native habitat it is subjected to more extremes of heat and coolness than other species.

S. pendula is still another trailing species but with nearly round gray-green foliage—flat and with serrated edges. Its medium lavender-blue flowers

appear singly or in clusters of two.

S. pusilla is the smallest of the species and a true miniature. Leaves have purple undersides, and its tiny flowers are bicolored—upper lobes are blue but lower lobes are white.

S. shumensis is another miniature which forms many crowns of small, almost round olive-green leaves. Its small flowers are nearly white with contrasting violet centers. Because its native habitat is quite dry, this species is sensitive to overwatering.

S. tongwensis is another like *S. confusa* which can be grown as a single-crowned plant but with a definite tendency, then, to lean over and grow toward the pot's edge. The large, somewhat heart-shaped leaves have a dintinctive lighter central streak; light blue flowers are profusely produced.

S. velutina has velvety, scalloped, heart-shaped leaves—dark green above and red-purple underneath. Above these are carried pale blue, dark-eyed flowers. Plants form very attractive, single-crowned and fairly flat rosettes. This species is also sensitive to overwatering.

WELL-GROWN specimen African violets can contribute beautiful accents to interior decoration, or they may be individual showpieces. Plants above are Rhapsodie 'Sophia' and Rhapsodie 'Gigi'; below is 'Wedgewood.'

SHADING PLANTS *from direct sunlight during hottest months will be necessary. In the home (above) you can use curtains that filter the light; commercial operations (below) whitewash the greenhouse glass.*

Simple Guidelines for Healthy Growth

EW PEOPLE want to grow African violets only for their leaves. While the foliage itself is undeniably attractive on a well-grown plant, the beauty most of us seek is in the charming, colorful flowers.

Bringing African violets into flower does not depend on secret knowledge or the proverbial "green thumb." Rather, it involves an understanding of basic and simple cultural needs. However, even under seemingly ideal conditions a plant sometimes will be reluctant to bloom, but this can often be explained by the fact that some African violets are more free with their blooms than are others. Often those that have fewer flowers will compensate by having flowers larger than the usual, while others may bloom profusely for a few months and then rest a few months.

It is difficult to know what a plant's blooming habits are until you have grown it for a while. Give a plant good culture and a fair trial before judging it a shy bloomer. If, however, a plant fails to reward you with flowers after many months of good care, you probably would be happier replacing it with another variety which might be more generous with its blooms.

LOCATION AND CARE

Although freedom of flowering may vary from variety to variety and, in addition, will depend upon a plant's maturity, there are a number of cultural guidelines which you should follow in order to promote the best possible performance from a plant.

Light

All plants must have light to survive, and African violets are no exception. While they will grow in a northern exposure, there you will probably have only leaves and no bloom. Generally, African violets need all the light they can get throughout the year except in summer when full sun may be too intense. In spring, fall, and winter, several hours of sun daily are desirable for healthy, blooming plants. It is easy to tell when plants have too much sun: Foliage turns yellow and leaf edges burn. Too little light produces lovely dark green foliage but few, if any, flowers. Therefore, seek the happy medium. A western exposure is good all year for most African violets.

Any window in the home that offers some light (if not totally darkened by trees or buildings) is a potential location for plants. If direct sunlight through a window is diffused somewhat by tree branches this is an ideal exposure. Light that comes through textured glass is also good. In these situations the light will be enough to keep plants growing but not so bright as to burn leaves. If your African violets are at a south-facing window, keep a thin curtain between the pane of glass and the plants during late spring and summer.

Turn plants a complete 360 degrees every month so that all leaves will receive equal shares of light; an easy way to do this is to give plants a quarter turn each week, always turning in the same direction. Without this turning a plant's symmetry will be spoiled as the leaves constantly receiving the most light will grow larger, longer, and more rapidly than leaves on the plant's shaded side.

If you have no window space that would provide proper light, you might want to try growing African violets under artificial light. See pages 32–36 for specific directions.

Temperature and Ventilation

In the home, African violets will be comfortable if you are. A daytime temperature of 72°–75° is fine; night temperatures should be in the low 60's. A variation between day and night temperature is essential if you want healthy plants. Excessive heat will harm African violets, so on hot summer days see that your plants occupy the coolest place possible. Likewise, extreme cold will damage plants, so in winter keep them away from windowpanes to avoid temperatures that would go below 55°.

Along with comfortable temperatures, African violets need a well-ventilated growing area. The stagnant air of a closed room only invites ill health

and second-rate performance. Direct air currents on plants can, however, be as detrimental as no air movement. The best solution is to provide indirect ventilation—an open window in an adjoining room, or an open window in the same room but far enough from plants that drafts won't reach them. In winter when windows are generally shut, use a small electric fan operating at low speed to keep air moving.

In the zeal of plant collecting it is tempting to gather together as many plants as you can squeeze into a given area. However, just as African violet plants need air circulating in the room, each plant needs air circulating around it. Resist the inclination to crowd plants together and, instead, consider an artificial light garden if you have more plants than the available window space can accommodate.

Watering

Frequently the novice African violet grower wastes much anxiety over when and how to water his plants. The simplest guidelines are these: *When* depends on the size of the pot, the weather, and the plant itself. *How*—from top or bottom—depends on your own taste. The one invariable direction is that you must use water which is approximately at room temperature. Cold water has a particularly shocking effect on plants—they may respond by developing leaf spot or by refusing to develop new buds. The easiest way to get room-temperature water without resorting to thermometers is simply to draw the water and let it stand overnight in the same room as the plants before using it.

Bottom watering—putting water in the saucer and letting the soil in the pot soak it up by capillary action—is advocated by many growers, primarily because it is easy and it avoids the possibility of getting water into a plant's crown. However, top watering—if done carefully so that only the soil is moistened—is not only just as effective, it is sometimes necessary in a bottom-watered collection. When water is taken up into the soil by capillary action, any salts in the water (and the fertilizer salts in the liquid preparations) will gradually accumulate in the soil to the point that eventually they could damage roots. In addi-

PLASTIC POTS are easy to handle, but hold moisture so well that you must be careful not to over-water plants.

TOP WATERING is easy if you have long-spouted watering can to put water under leaves, onto soil.

tion, accumulated salts on the soil surface can cause stem rot. The only way to get rid of these salts before they build up to damaging concentrations is to periodically leach them from the soil by applying water from the top and letting it run through the soil and out the pot's drainage hole. If you regularly water your African violets from the bottom, a thorough once-a-month top watering should be sufficient.

Watering from the top requires more care and time than bottom watering, as it is difficult—particularly with large mature plants—to hit only the soil and not get water into the plants' crowns. Use a long-spouted watering can (rather than a pitcher, for example) for the greatest accuracy when applying water from the top.

It is difficult to set up rigid watering schedules for all plants. Generally, water African violets in 5 or 6-inch pots about three times a week in dull weather. Smaller pots will need water more often. Never allow soil to become soggy; it should be kept evenly moist. When the soil surface begins to feel dry to the touch it is time to apply more water.

Strongly alkaline (hard) water is not good for most plants. If your area has hard water—as in many parts of the Southwest—this condition can be alleviated by a solution of one tablespoon of vinegar in one gallon of water. Use this once a month in place of a regular watering and it will help reduce accumulated alkalinity in the potting soil.

The other extreme—water that has been softened artificially with sodium—may be fatal to plants in time. For sodium-treated water there is no corrective measure as there is for hard water. If you can't draw water before it is softened, your recourse is to use rainwater or bottled water.

Self-watering containers and wick-fed pots are convenient innovations for indoor gardeners and they are especially a boon for the person who must be away from his African violets for days at a time. The different manufacturers of these containers offer different designs, but basically most units operate with a spun glass wick that draws water by capillary action through the drainage hole into the soil. As the water is used, you add more water to the reservoir.

Fertilizing

As plants grow, their roots deplete the soil of available nutrients. Consequently, to maintain healthy, even growth you will have to fertilize your African violets periodically. The three major elements most needed for healthy growth—nitrogen, phosphorus, and potassium—are available in commercial fertilizers. The fertilizer labels will state the percentages of these valuable elements—such as 10-10-5, 20-10-10, and so on, with nitrogen listed first and phosphorus and potash following in that order.

Organic fertilizers such as fish emulsion, animal manure, bone meal, blood meal, or hoof and horn meal can also be used for fertilizing, alternating with a complete balanced commercial formulation.

You can purchase fertilizer that is made specifically for African violets: be sure to read all labels carefully to select a moderate strength fertilizer with a formula of about 10-10-5. Fertilizers with too much nitrogen will give you handsome robust plants, but there will be little bloom.

Commercial fertilizers come in liquid or granular form. The liquids and many granular types are to be mixed with water; some granular or pelletized fertilizers can be applied directly to the soil where regular waterings will dissolve them. Generally, use a little less than the label recommends to avoid any possibility of burning the plants. Fertilize your African violets about once a month throughout the spring, summer, and fall, not at all in the winter. Whenever you fertilize, be sure the soil is moist before you apply the solution.

While fertilizing is intended to benefit plants, it can also be harmful if used at inopportune times. For example, after a plant has had a big burst of flowers, let it rest; don't fertilize it and try to force it back into bloom again right away. And never fertilize sick or newly potted plants.

Pots and Potting

A few years ago there were perhaps a dozen varieties of containers for plants; today there are hundreds. While African violets can be grown in almost any container, the standard, time-tested clay pots are still best because water evaporates slowly through the material. Many plastic pots perhaps look more attractive, but they will keep soil moist longer than clay pots will, and this prolonged moistness can lead to crown rot if you water too often. Should you decide to use plastic pots, plant your African violets in a soil mixture that is very coarse and porous (see page 19).

Glazed pottery pots are also available but many of these do not have drainage holes through which any excess water can escape. If you try to grow African violets in such drainless pots, you generally end up with soggy soil which eventually means death for the plant. If you seek the decorative effect of the glazed pot and want to use it as it is, slip an African violet in a clay pot into the glazed container rather than potting the plant directly in it. Of course, if you have a drainage hole drilled in the bottom of a glazed pot (most stores which sell glass will be able to do this for you), you can plant your African violet directly in it, observing the same precautions you would when using a plastic container.

Novelty containers such as strawberry jars also

YOU CAN DRILL holes in some drainless pots. Brace inside of bottom with wood block, then drill.

will grow and display African violets well. Most of them have drainage holes; if they do not, you can have holes drilled just as you would for glazed ceramic pots.

Generally, single-crown African violet plants are intolerant of large containers; the soil that is not occupied by roots can become soggy and sour, a condition which can lead to eventual crown rot. Most African violets seem to bear a better crop of flowers in "tight" pots—pots that are just large enough to accommodate their root system. So use the smallest sized pot that will hold the plant and still be in proportion to it. Seedlings should go into 2 1/4-inch pots and be shifted to a 3 or 4-inch pot in about nine months. Mature specimen plants with a 7 or 8-inch leaf spread are best in 5 or 6-inch pots.

First, be sure to thoroughly clean old pots before you use them again. It's a good idea to immerse them in boiling water for a few minutes to sterilize them; then scour pots to remove dirt and crusted salt deposits. Let new clay pots soak in water for a few hours so they will absorb water and therefore not draw moisture from the soil when you water your newly potted plant. On plastic pots use hot water and a detergent; scrub them carefully to remove all old soil, then let them dry.

To remove a plant from an old container, slip your hand under the rosette of leaves (with your palm down—against the soil surface) and hold the plant's crown between two fingers; then turn the pot upside down and tap it sharply against a table edge. Try to ease the plant from its container; do not pull but rather tease it loose. You should end up with the root ball and soil in the palm of your hand, the plant against the back of your hand (see the photograph on this page). If it still does not come out, take a knife and run it around the inside of the pot between pot and soil, then repeat the process just described. When you get the African violet out of its pot, crumble away old soil with your fingers or run a pencil through it to loosen compacted soil. Trim away all dead, brown roots.

Place a curved piece of broken pottery (curved side facing upward) over the new pot's drainage hole before adding new soil. Then put in a mound of your potting soil and center the plant on it. If the plant sits too low in the pot,

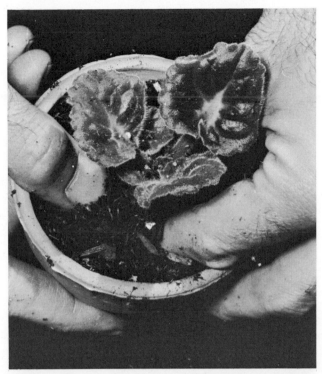

SMALL POTS *are best for small plants. New plants and seedlings need only 2-3-inch pots.*

REMOVE PLANT *from its container so that root ball is held in palm of your hand, leaves are undamaged.*

ROOT BALL should hold together if plant is rootbound and needing larger container.

lift it out and add more soil to bring it up to the proper level; if the plant is too high, take away some soil. After you have the plant positioned, fill in and around with additional potting soil; rap the bottom of the pot sharply on the table to settle the soil, and firm the soil with a blunt stick—or your fingers or thumbs, if you can do this without damaging the leaves. Fill the container with soil to within half an inch of the pot's rim; this will allow space for water when you top-water your plants. Thoroughly soak the newly-potted plant, let it drain, and then resoak the soil. Set the plant in a protected, somewhat shaded area and water only moderately for a few weeks; just keep the soil barely moist. Then move the African violet to its permanent place and follow a regular watering schedule.

If you delay repotting too long, faster growing varieties will form a "trunk" above soil level where old leaves have fallen off. When repotting, bury this trunk up to the lowest leaves, and new roots will form along it (in time, old roots shrivel and die). You also can sever the roots from the trunk and re-root the plant in water.

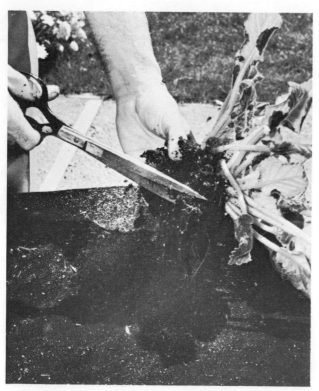

CAREFULLY CRUMBLE soil of old root ball to free roots, then trim any dead or decayed roots.

GENTLY FIRM new soil around plant roots in new container, then water plant thoroughly.

Soil

When you buy soil for your African violets, feel it; it should be porous, almost fluffy. It should never be heavy or sticky because then when it is wet it will be impervious to air and roots will not be able to grow satisfactorily. Almost all African violets will fare well in the time-tested standard mix for house plants: one-third garden loam, one-third leafmold, and one-third sand. This is a light mixture that will retain water long enough for health but not so long that it might harm roots.

There are, almost literally, as many potting mixtures for African violets as there are African violet growers. A variation of the above mixture is two parts leafmold or peatmoss, and two parts garden loam, mixed with one part vermiculite. To this combination some growers add a handful of sand, some perlite, and a sprinkling of charcoal chips. What you ultimately use depends on what will grow plants best for you. Just remember that soil *must* be light and porous.

No matter what soil you choose it should be sterilized (or, more properly, pasteurized). Packaged soil mixes come already sterilized. If you buy one of these, look for those especially formulated for African violets. If you use garden soil in a soil preparation you'll have to sterilize it yourself. The oven method is a simple, but smelly, procedure: Mix together the ingredients in a large pan; add enough water to saturate the mix, cover it, and bake in an oven at 190°–210° for at least two hours. Then cool the mixture and air it for three or more days before planting in it, stirring it several times during this period.

Some specially-formulated African violet potting mixtures contain no soil. In these soilless mediums, plants will need fertilizer more often than will plants grown in mixes that contain soil—particularly if the soilless preparation drains rapidly and retains little moisture. If you buy plants already potted, ask what kind of mixture they are planted in for.an indication of fertilizer and water needs.

Vacationing Plants

What do you do with African violet plants at vacation time? If you are going away only for a few days, most African violets will survive without any special consideration. If you are going to be gone a week or more, perhaps a friend can come in and water them for you. Of course, plants in self-watering containers will get along with no attention.

Should you have to leave your African violets entirely on their own for a few weeks, put them in a bright place (but without direct sun) where temperatures will remain on the cool side of their preferred range. Then moisten soil and cover the plants with polyethylene plastic sheeting, or cover individual plants with plastic bags. This helps to preserve humidity and keep soil moist. Before covering plants with plastic, remove all flowers and buds that are large enough to open while you will be gone. Flowers that decay on leaves in high humidity may provide a breeding ground for fungus spores.

Another vacation treatment for African violets is to put plants in a cardboard box filled with moist sphagnum moss. Pack the plants close together in the moss, but be sure there is adequate ventilation in the growing area. This should keep plants moist as long as the sphagnum stays damp.

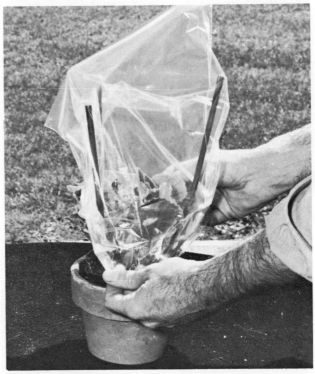

PLASTIC BAG keeps plant moist enough that you can leave it unattended for short period.

PLANT PROBLEMS

Like all plants, African violets have their share of possible problems, although in varying degrees. Some growers never see a mite or an aphid; others are not so fortunate. The best advice is still that an ounce of prevention *is* worth a pound of cure. Applied to African violets this means that you should observe your plants: Inspect leaves and stems frequently to catch any trouble before it starts. A mild insect infestation is easy to remedy; once pests get a foothold, eliminating them becomes a more difficult task.

Insects

The common plant insects that you may have occasion to eradicate are: aphids, mealybug, thrips, black fly, soil mealybug, and cyclamen mite. If you catch them before they have a chance to get a foothold, they are easy to eliminate.

Aphids are small, soft-bodied insects, usually black or green, that accumulate on new growth and suck out vital plant juices. *Control:* Wash them off daily with lukewarm water; if infestation is severe, use a rotenone or pyrethrum spray, or—of the more toxic sprays—malathion, diazinon, or a systemic.

Mealybugs —soft, cottony-white insects—lodge themselves in leaf axils and undersides of leaves, occasionally deep in the crown of the plant. They suck vital plant juices and can destroy a plant if not eliminated in time. *Control:* Rub them off the plant with an alcohol-dipped cotton swab, then carefully wash the plant in lukewarm water. Repeat this operation daily until all newly hatched mealybugs are destroyed. Toxic materials which are effective are: malathion, diazinon, and the systemics.

Soil mealybugs are insidious because they do their work underground and can go undetected for a long time. If a plant appears wilted or stunted, soil mealybugs may be at work. They destroy the root tips so that a plant becomes unable to take in water and fertilizers in solution. To be sure, remove the plant from its pot and examine the root ball; if you see grayish-white bugs on the surface of the root ball you'll know this is the problem. *Control:* The best control is prevention—plant only in sterilized soil. If you have an infested plant that you must save, a systemic insecticide is your best remedy.

Scale is an infrequent offender but may be found occasionally on some gesneriads. It is a small, waxy, flattened disk-shaped insect, usually some shade of tan to yellow, often accompanied by a black, sticky exudate. *Control:* Remove scale with a toothpick or toothbrush dipped in mild detergent and lukewarm water; then wash leaves with clear, lukewarm water. Toxic sprays that are effective are malathion, diazinon, or the systemics.

Thrips are tiny (almost microscopic), slender insects, pale yellow when young and brown when mature, that move about rapidly when disturbed. They can cause premature bud drop and streaking of flower petals, and a white stippling on leaves. *Control:* The same sprays that control aphids will eradicate an infestation of thrips. Removal of all flowers and buds helps eliminate a primary source of infestation.

Mites are minute insects, several kinds of which can be troublesome for many different plants. Cyclamen mite probably is the most serious pest of gesneriads, especially dangerous because the mites cannot be seen without the aid of a magnifying lens. Only when you see evidence of their damage—distorted, twisted foliage, streaked flowers, and stunted growth—do you know they're there. The first indications usually are in the center of a plant: The crown appears lighter than the rest of the leaves, the small leaves there become grayish or yellow-green, and they remain small and twisted. If you notice cobwebs on flowers or leaves and if foliage is at all brown or stippled, then red spider mites are at work. If broad mite attacks a plant, the leaves usually will curl down (if it is cyclamen mite they will curl up). *Control:* First, isolate your mite-infested plants from those which appear to be clean. Then, treat the infested plants with diazinon or one of the systemics. You can use these as sprays or you may immerse the plants in a spray solution (after first covering the soil surface so that soil will not unnecessarily cloud the solution). Especially if you dip the plants, wear protective gloves so that toxic solution does not contact your skin. Usually several treatments, spaced about a week apart, will be necessary to clean up an infestation.

Nematodes are soil pests—fine, threadlike, parasitic worms that infest roots, causing a general debility which the plants reflect by assuming a sickly yellow-green color and a tired, drooping appearance. For definite evidence of nematodes, remove the ailing plant from its pot and examine its roots; if they show signs of swelling or if the stalk at the soil line is spongy, root-knot nematodes may be at work. *Control*: This involves working with nematocides (chemicals which will kill nematodes). These are toxic materials which must be handled with extreme care, particularly if you use them indoors in a confined area. Even if you use a nematocide the chances for a plant's recovery are slim. The safest remedy is to discard the infested plant. The best nematode *prevention* is to use only sterilized potting soil.

Insecticides

You will find many insecticides at your local nursery or garden supply center. Some are formulated to kill specific pests (such as mites or aphids); many preparations are made for specific plants such as roses or African violets. In this arsenal of weapons against bugs, the poisons are classed as: contact insecticides that destroy by touching the insect; systemics that are absorbed into the structure of the plant, killing the pest after it ingests the plant's poisoned cell sap; and stomach poisons, sprayed onto the plant, which kill pests after they ingest the poison. Especially in the home, you should always use extreme caution if you decide to use any of these toxic materials.

Observation is the best weapon against insects and disease. Any mild infestation usually can be eradicated with home remedies. These include hand-picking of insects, washing plants with warm water, or using cotton swabs dipped in alcohol for control of mealybugs or aphids.

However, if insects do get a foothold and you must resort to toxic controls, first use the less toxic poisons such as pyrethrum and rotenone. These are botanical insecticides (derived from plant extracts) that will control aphids, thrips, and mealybugs. For severe insect infestations use diazinon or malathion or one of the systemics; these are the safest of the more highly toxic insecticides for use around humans and pets. Always follow carefully the directions on an insecticide's label.

EASILY-RECOGNIZED PESTS or their symptoms include these three. Cyclamen mite shows in damaged leaves; mealybug (enlarged) is cottony and white; nematodes produce swollen roots.

Diseases

In contrast to insects—which can invade perfectly healthy collections—most diseases will be avoided if you have your plants in congenial locations and give them regular attention. In fact, only virus infections are beyond your control. Of the diseases in the following list, crown rot is the most frequently encountered—and one of the easiest to prevent.

Botrytis blight is a gray mold that turns blooms and buds into mushy, brown tissue. Epidemics develop under cool, moist conditions with high humidity. Most often the fungus enters the plant through dead or dying flowers or leaves, but when conditions are right it will infect live tissue. *Control*: Be sure plants have good air circulation, avoid high humidity and overfertilization with nitrogen. At the first sign of infection, remove dead plant parts and parts attacked by botrytis, then apply a fungicide such as captan, thiram, or ferbam. Isolate infected plants until you are sure the disease is under control.

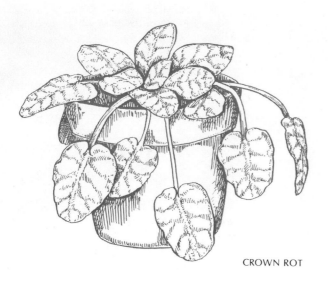

CROWN ROT

Crown rot is indicated if a healthy plant suddenly starts wilting. This disease most often gets its start in plants that are erratically watered so that their root environment alternates between desert and bog conditions. *Control*: Avoid overwatering (with the resulting soggy soil) and avoid alternating extremes of wetness and dryness in the potting soil. Also be careful, when watering, to keep water from settling in the crown of the plant. If crown rot develops but has not progressed to the fatal point, repot the plant. First remove it from its container, shake off all soil, and remove dead roots and soft stems; apply sulfur to all areas where you have cut out rotten tissue. Then repot the plant into a seedling soil mixture of potting soil and vermiculite or perlite—and hope for the best.

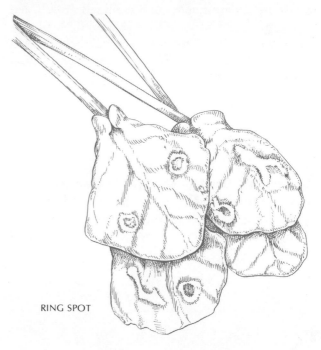

RING SPOT

Ring spot usually appears as yellow rings on the upper leaf surfaces and is generally caused by cold water coming in contact with soil or foliage. Sunlight on wet leaves also can cause ring spot. *Control*: Use only tepid water when watering your African violets, and keep water off leaf surfaces if they will be exposed to sunlight.

Viruses (such as tobacco mosaic, for example) occasionally attack various gesneriads. Their presence is easy to identify: streaked, distorted leaves, sometimes with irregular yellow spots, on a plant generally lacking in vigor. Usually viruses are spread by mites or other insect vectors, although gardeners sometimes aid their spread when they use a cutting tool on an infected plant and then use the same tool on an uninfected plant. Viruses are systemic—that is, they are contained in a plant's cell sap. *Control*: There is no effective cure for virus, so infected plants should be removed from a collection and destroyed.

Physiological Problems

While insects can be responsible for the decline of a plant, many times cultural conditions may be at fault, instead. The information in the accompanying chart will help you to determine if pests are at work or if your plants' problems stem from growing conditions.

Symptoms	Possible Cause	Remedy
Weak stems, smaller leaves than normal, flowering sparse or not at all	Insufficient light	Move plant to a better lighted window or set up a fluorescent light garden
Leaves have dull brown edges, flowers are smaller than normal	Insufficient humidity	Place pots on trays or plant saucers filled with gravel and water
Soft, rapid growth and lack of flowers	Temperature too high	Move to a room where temperature stays between 62° and 75°.
Growth slow and leaves curl downward	Temperature too low	Move to a room where temperature stays between 62° and 75°.
Leaves become yellow, growth is small, and flowers are smaller than normal	Insufficient fertilizing	Try fertilizing plants twice a month
Leaves dark green but flowers few	Too much fertilizing	Fertilize half as often as usual, and use a fertilizer lower in nitrogen
Leaves drop or flower buds drop off	Sudden temperature change	Move plants to a location not subject to rapid changes
Leaves become brittle, brown	Soil is deficient in nutrients	Repot plant if soil is old, and begin regular fertilizing
Leaves develop brown spots	Plants watered with cold water	Always use room-temperature water
Bleached, tired looking foliage	Too much light	Remove plants from direct sunlight

Words to the Wise . . .

To avoid any problems with African violets, you should observe a few basic rules no matter how foolish they may seem when you have what appears to be a perfectly healthy plant:

- Isolate new plants from your others for at least a month; two months would be even better. During this period, observe them closely for the presence of any insects.
- Be wary of introducing plants other than African violets into your collection; they may carry diseases or insects that also will affect African violets. (If you do add other plants—other gesneriads, for example—follow the isolation procedure mentioned above.)
- Plant only in sterilized soil.
- If a plant begins to sulk (if leaves go limp or if spots develop on leaf-stems), immediately remove it from the vicinity of your other plants.
- After handling an infected plant, always wash your hands thoroughly.

ADAPTABILITY *is one key to the popularity of African violets—as long as they receive proper light and temperature. Traditional window display (above) shows off several plants as does the bowlful below—each one in its own pot.*

Versatile Plants for Indoor Decoration

THE VIRTUES of African violets as indoor decoration lie in their combination of beauty and versatility. Truly, African violets come close to being an all-purpose decorating item. You will find them used effectively *en masse* at windows, under artificial lights in a sunless part of a room, grouped on plant stands, in terrariums, or simply as cheerful accents on coffee tables, in entry halls, or on well-lighted kitchen counters—to mention only a few possibilities. For an effective mass display (good as a table centerpiece, for example), try grouping several pots of blooming African violets in a large, shallow container such as a metal bowl. Or, for eye-level enjoyment, grow a few African violets in hanging baskets or suspended pots. There are even trailing varieties that are especially suited to hanging display—indoors at windows or outdoors (in spring and summer) from porch eaves and rafters.

Unlike many other house plants that eventually may outgrow their allotted spaces, African violets will remain a predictable size and are easily moved to any suitable location in the home. The only danger is that you may be tempted to grow more than you have room for!

WINDOW DISPLAYS

Before the advent of fluorescent lights, a window was the only place where you could grow African violets. Naturally, window displays have always been popular—there, plants are assured of receiving adequate light and they can be viewed easily—and windows continue to be the most frequently used staging for amateur growers with moderate-sized collections.

There are many possibilities for shelf arrangements that will hold plants at windows; the choice is largely a matter of personal taste and ingenuity. For standard window sizes you often can buy pre-cut and packaged glass shelves with the necessary brackets to hold them up. If your windows are odd sizes you can still purchase brackets separately and have shelves cut to fit out of ¼-inch plate glass. Shelves of wood are even easier to install because you can do whatever cutting and fitting is necessary. As a rule-of-thumb example, three shelves, each 24 inches long and 8 inches wide, will give you space for about eighteen African violets without crowding. You'll probably want to have each pot sitting in its own saucer; this will protect shelves and windowsills from water stains and will prevent water from dropping off shelves onto plants below.

Where existing window sills are not wide enough for plants but the light is good, you might use portable plant stands, tea carts, or narrow tables placed by the windows to gain space for your potted plants. If you use portable stands or carts you can easily move your blooming African violets from room to room whenever you want a temporary display of color.

HANGING GARDENS

Although you have not nearly as many varieties from which to choose as you do from the lists of the usual rosette-forming plants, there are some African Violets which have a trailing growth

HANGING CONTAINER shows off trailing African violet; soon stems will grow over pot's edge.

habit. These are tailor-made for showing off in hanging pots or baskets. But even if you don't have one of the trailing sorts, a large multiple-crowned plant of any of the usual types can put on a spectacular show when suspended at eye-level. With nothing close to crowd them, these hanging plants are bound to enjoy good air circulation.

Hanging plants can be suspended in two ways: The basket or pot is attached to at least two wires, cords, or chains which are connected to a hook or eye inserted in the ceiling; or, the hanging container is held up by a wall-mounted bracket. The latter can be easily attached to a window frame; then you simply hang the pot from the bracket.

You will find a wide assortment of containers in which you can grow plants for hanging. Some containers are specifically designed for hanging, while others can be adapted easily to the purpose. There are manufactured wire attachments, for example, which will attach to a standard clay pot and allow you to suspend it; even better are the devices which attach to the pot's saucer (you then just set the pot in the saucer) so that watering the hanging plant entails no mess from water dripping onto the floor beneath. Glazed ceramic pots often are especially decorative hanging accents, but for those that have no drainage holes you will want to keep your African violet plants in standard clay pots and slip them inside the glazed ceramic ones.

Inexpensive wire or wire mesh baskets can be used to feature hanging African violets but not without this special preparation: first, line the basket with a layer of sphagnum moss so the potting soil will be contained in the basket. Add the potting soil (and then the plant) only after the sphagnum liner has been firmed in place. You'll probably have to pay more close attention to watering African violets in wire baskets than you would plants in other containers, since the sphagnum lining (rather than the sides of a ceramic or plastic pot) is all that comes between potting soil and air. Unless the floor beneath wire baskets is of a material that is not bothered by water, you'll have to take the baskets down and water them at the sink whenever they need it; otherwise water will drain through the sphagnum and onto the floor below.

LIKE A JEWEL in an expensive setting, this African violet sparkles inside its glass bubble bowl. Soil and atmospheric moisture promote healthy growth.

African violets in hanging baskets are always on display, which means that grooming is particularly important for these plants. For best appearance at all times, be sure to remove all dead and declining flowers and leaves.

AFRICAN VIOLETS IN GLASS GARDENS

Miniature greenhouses are what you're giving your African violets when you plant them in glass vessels such as bubble bowls, bottles, brandy snifters, apothecary jars, and the like. And when grown "under glass" the plants almost never suffer from lack of moisture or humidity. With the larger glass bowls, jars, or bottles you can even try your hand at creating miniature landscapes, featuring African violets but including other compatible plants as well. The combination of sparkling glass encasing a robust blooming plant is invariably a showpiece.

Miniature and semi-miniature African violet varieties are ideal choices for growing in glass containers, for even with such congenial moisture and humidity they still will not be likely to outgrow the confines of the glass vessel. In fact, the miniatures may actually grow better in a glass enclosure because the soil moisture will fluctuate much more slowly than it does in the very small pots which miniatures require.

Even if you decide to grow only miniature African violets in this manner, you should choose a glass container that is at least 8 inches across at its widest point. This is about the smallest size that will accommodate miniatures without appearing to cramp them.

With glass bowls, jars, or bottles there will be no drainage holes for water to escape. Therefore, preparation of the potting soil—as well as subsequent watering—will have to be done with special care. Be sure the potting soil is sterilized; either buy a sterilized prepared mixture or prepare your own according to the directions on page 19. Whatever mixture you use it should be one that will not become soggy and dense. Before planting, first place a 1-inch layer of charcoal

MINIATURE AFRICAN VIOLETS

You will find that a number of nurseries specialize in or at least feature miniature African violets. These are perfect replicas or regular-sized varieties, yet are small enough that a 2½-inch pot is the largest they will need. To the collector, one advantage to the miniatures is that more varieties can be accommodated in a given space.

Because the small pots miniatures need will dry out so quickly, it often is easier (and wiser) to group several small plants together in a larger container such as a shallow bonsai dish or a clay azalea pot. Be sure the container has a drainage hole. With several plants sharing a larger soil mass, watering is easier and you need not fear that plants will dry out rapidly. Potting soils and planting are no different from directions described on pages 16-19.

If you prefer to keep your miniatures in their individual small containers but want a way to keep soil from drying out quickly, sink several potted miniatures in a large container of sterilized potting soil and keep this soil moist too.

Be cautious of putting miniature African violets in tea cups and other decorative small containers that have no drainage holes, as soggy soil conditions will easily harm plants with such small root systems. For really best results—and an outstanding display for them—try growing your miniatures in small "greenhouses": bubble bowls, jars, decanters, and snifters. This is described on page 29. Surrounded by glass, the plants are protected from drafts and fluctuating temperatures, and the increased humidity within the container will produce healthier plants. Another advantage: moisture condensing inside the glass container helps water the plants.

Miniature African violet 'Dolly Dimple'

and gravel on the bottom; then cover this with at least 3 inches of soil and plant your African violet. Carefully firm the potting soil around the plant roots and water lightly—just enough to provide good contact between potting soil and roots.

Watering is most easily done with a watering can that has a long, slender spout. With this, you can direct the water just onto the soil, keeping glass and plant free of water marks or splashed soil. Remember, you don't want soil to be really wet but rather just moderately moist.

Set your garden in glass where it will receive good light but never direct sunlight, as sun coming through glass will easily burn plants.

Fertilize only when plants show definite signs that they need it. Obviously you want them to bloom well, but you don't want them to quickly and exuberantly outgrow the limits of their glass enclosure.

SIMPLE MINIATURE LANDSCAPE contains only a hollowed-out rock, miniature African violet.

Miniature landscapes, using miniature African violets and other small companion plants, can be staged attractively in larger glass containers like aquariums. Here, you can create replicas of natural scenes but in diminutive proportions, making small hills and valleys, using small stones and gravel to imitate natural rock outcroppings and dry stream beds. Some small plants to use with your African violets in these landscapes are: small ferns and palms; mosses, liverworts, and lichens; *Fittonia verschaffeltii; Maranta leuconeura; Pilea involucrata;* and *Soleirolia soleirolii* (baby's tears).

Soil preparation and planting for miniature landscapes is no different from the basic methods just described.

Bottle gardens offer the same cultural and decorative advantages as do gardens in brandy snifters, bubble bowls, and aquariums. The difference is that it is more difficult to plant and maintain bottle gardens simply because of the small opening through which you have to work.

Soil for bottle gardens should be the same as for the other glass-enclosed plantings, and preparation for planting differs in only one respect. You will want to keep the inside walls of the bottle entirely free of soil particles; to do this, make a slender funnel, long enough to reach nearly to the bottom of the bottle, from a sheet of stiff paper. Then pour drainage material and soil through it.

Planting is best done using a length of flexible copper tubing, a pronged wooden stick, or a 12-inch-long glass pipette—any of which will reach through the neck of the bottle and down to the soil to help position the plant. If you use a glass pipette, work a piece of rubber tubing onto the end to provide a flexible tip. First, make a hole for the plant's roots in the soil mixture; then carefully ease the plant—roots first—down through the bottle's neck and into the hole, using the sticks or tubing as tweezers. When the plant is positioned, use the end of the rod or stick to tamp the soil down around the roots.

An easier approach to bottle gardening (although results are longer in coming) is to sow African violet seeds directly on the soil in the bottle. Then, as the seeds germinate, thin out the plants until only a few remain. As these come into bloom you may want to remove all but the most attractive specimen.

BOOKSHELF BECOMES PLANTER after installation of fluorescent lights (concealed behind facing strip attached to shelf edge). Shelves adjust for proper light distance from plants.

ARTIFICIAL LIGHT GARDENS

Your African violet collection need not be limited by the availability of well-lighted window space. You can have thriving plants almost anywhere in your home if you use artificial light to illuminate a growing area. African violets are among the most rewarding plants to grow under artificial light. First of all, their light requirements are not excessive; two 40-watt fluorescent tubes, going for 12 hours a day, will accommodate 9–12 plants. Furthermore, African violets are neutral day-length plants—that is, they do not require a specific number of hours of darkness or of light to bloom, but will do so instead under a wide range of day lengths. Since you will not be restricted to space at or near windows, the artificial-light growing area can be anywhere in the house: an unused book shelf, a room divider planter, part of the garage, a basement, a space over the kitchen counter—any spot that would be improved by the addition of growing plants.

All plants grown under artificial light respond best to the light quality that most closely approximates natural light. From sunlight, plants use chiefly the red and blue radiant energy from opposite ends of the light spectrum—and about twice as much red light as blue. Red light stimulates vegetative growth; blue light regulates the respiratory process.

One way to provide the essential light for growth is to use a combination of ordinary natural-white and daylight-type fluorescent lights. Allow 15–20 watts of light for each square foot of growing area—so that two 40-watt lamps, for example, are all you would need for a 4-foot-square area such as a 1 x 4-foot shelf.

Incandescent lights usually are not strong enough in the red or blue areas of the light spectrum, they generate too much heat for tender plant leaves, and they deliver only about a third as much light for the same amount of electricity as do fluorescent lights. However, some growers feel that using an incandescent bulb of low wattage does aid plant growth. If you try this, use one 8-watt incandescent bulb for each 40-watt

TABLE-TOP fluorescent fixture converts any flat surface into a growing area. An advantage to this type unit is that it can be moved easily to a new location.

fluorescent tube, and place it at least 18 inches above plants to forestall any damage from the heat they emit.

Several manufacturers of electric lights and fixtures have developed fluorescent tubes designed especially for growing plants indoors. Each tube combines a high intensity of light at both the red and blue ends of the light spectrum. Some growers use these tubes exclusively, while others use them in combination with the standard fluorescent tubes. These special tubes are available in standard fluorescent lamp sizes from 24 inches to 96 inches long and will fit into ordinary fluorescent fixtures.

When you purchase a fluorescent light unit you probably will have a choice of preheat tubes or rapid start types. Preheat tubes will have a longer life than the rapid start, and they also are less expensive. Rapid start tubes occasionally balk where the humidity is high.

No matter which type of fluorescent tube you choose, you also will need a reflector. This is a canopy which throws light back onto the plants.

SIDE VIEW of above unit. Strap iron frame holds 48-inch industrial fluorescent fixture.

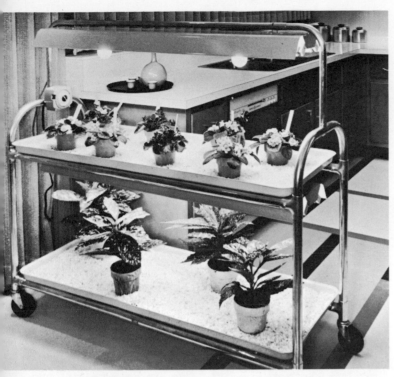

PORTABLE LIGHT GARDEN is manufactured metal unit on wheels for quick display in any room.

Most fluorescent light units come with reflectors attached.

The lifetime of a fluorescent tube varies according to its use. Also, the number of times that lights are turned on and off will affect their life span. It is a good practice to replace the tubes about every six months, before their output begins to decline appreciably. When black rings form at the ends of regular fluorescent tubes this indicates it is time to replace them.

Cultural Tips

Growing African violets under fluorescent lights is in some ways easier than growing them in natural light, the chief advantage being that you have greater control over their environment. Keep in mind, though, the following points as you plan and care for your illuminated garden.

Placement of plants. Dark foliage African violets need more light than do the lighter green and variegated sorts. Under standard white fluorescent lamps, place dark foliage varieties 10–12

inches below the tubes and directly under them; under tubes especially made for growing plants, the distance from the light source should be 12–14 inches—with placement still directly under the tubes. Varieties with light green or variegated leaves can be placed at the ends of the tubes and at the outer edges of the illuminated area; in both of these locations the light is less intense.

Too much light will cause plants to become unnaturally compact—bunched and tightened in the centers—and sometimes leaves will turn gray. With variegated varieties, too much light turns foliage solid green. Observe carefully the performance of your plants to determine if they are receiving too much or not enough light, then shift their positions accordingly.

Time and Temperature. In general, African violets need 10–12 hours daily of artificial light. To this rule, however, there are exceptions: Under the special lights for plants they will need only 8–10 hours a day; and in very hot weather the plants will perform better if you reduce the hours of illumination to about 8. It is helpful to install an inexpensive automatic timer to turn lights on and off on a regular schedule. These are particularly convenient whenever you have to leave your African violets unattended for any period of time.

Just as for African violets growing in natural light, plants under fluorescent lights need a lower nighttime temperature in order to put on their best performance. For example, if daytime temperature is around 72° then night temperature should be in the low 60's. Allow the temperature to go down gradually, as an abrupt change would be far more detrimental than no change at all. In most homes, nighttime temperature is naturally lower than that during the day, so you should need no special apparatus to control the change. However, if your plants are growing in a basement, garage, or other area not usually heated according to human needs then you will have to pay special attention to temperatures and their changes.

General care. African violets which grow at or near windows are still somewhat subject to the caprices of weather even though they are indoors. On cloudy days, when light intensity is reduced, plants grow less and transpire less; this reduces their need, on those days, for both water and nutrients. Under artificial lights, on the other

WELL LIGHTED table provides a congenial home for miniature streptocarpus plants growing in glass bubble bowls. Combination of good light and high humidity promotes optimum growth.

hand, your African violets will grow at a fairly constant rate every day, increasing their water and nutrient need and requiring both on a more regular schedule. You will have to check your plants to determine how often they need water (and this still will depend upon the size of the pot and whether it is porous or non-porous). But whatever your watering schedule is, you can use a soluble African violet fertilizer about every week to ten days throughout the year.

Finally, remember that ventilation and air circulation may assume even greater importance if you have your fluorescent light garden in an enclosed or windowless area where outside air currents (or just the movement of people) won't be available to keep air gently moving around plants. In such situations a small electric fan (but aimed *away* from the plants) running at low speed should keep the atmosphere from becoming stagnant. And along with this goes the same caution that applies to African violets in daylight locations: Don't crowd plants too closely together. If you find you have too many plants for one fluorescent light setup, then start another light garden to handle them.

HOME-MADE LIGHT GARDEN is constructed of redwood and 4-foot fluorescent fixtures.

COMMERCIAL PROPAGATION is a highly organized, carefully executed operation, but the methods are no different from ones you would use. New plants (top) are planted in prepared, sterilized soil mixture, then placed where they receive proper light and temperature (below).

Propagating Methods to Increase Your Collection

HAT NATURE IS a versatile performer is aptly demonstrated by the many ways in which African violets can be propagated. Few plants are less trouble to increase; even the novice African violet grower can raise new plants easily. The simplest method is to root leaves in water; it takes only a second to cut the leaf and put it into water—you need no special equipment. You can also divide multiple-crowned plants by separating the rosettes of leaves and planting each separately, and you can start new plants from suckers—the new shoots which grow from below the crown of a single-crowned plant. And, of course, you can start more plants by rooting leaves in your favorite potting mix, vermiculite, perlite, or other special rooting medium.

If you are slightly more ambitious and want lots of plants, you can sow seed and grow the seedlings on to blooming size. Sooner or later many African violet enthusiasts will want to propagate their very own African violets by hybridizing specific plants in their collection. Perhaps your seedlings will not surpass varieties already named, but each will be different (even if only slightly so) and you will have the satisfaction of knowing that these are your very own plants.

DIVIDE TO MULTIPLY

Many people increase their African violet collection without consciously planning to do so. Eventually a plant forms several crowns and gets too large for its container—so they pull off a crown and plant it separately. This is known as division. It takes only a few minutes and is almost always successful.

For best results, let the potting soil dry out somewhat before you attempt to divide your plant. Then remove it from the pot and study the plant's spread. With a multiple-crowned plant you will see separate clumps of leaves. Gently but firmly pull these sections apart, making sure to get roots with each division so the separated plants can re-establish themselves quickly. Put the divisions in 3-inch pots with fresh potting soil and water plants only moderately for the first few

OVERCROWDED *African violet has four crowns in one small pot; each crown is separate plant.*

SEPARATING *the four crowns gives you plants which are replanted individually in 3-inch pots.*

weeks. Keep the new divisions out of direct sunlight but in a bright place.

Frequently you will see fresh growth emerging below the crowns along the main "trunk." These are referred to as *suckers* and are another source of new plants. (Allowed to grow, they would be responsible for the multiple crowns in a multiple-crowned plant.) When they are large enough to handle, cut them from the main plant with a sharp, sterile knife. Rub the cut surfaces—both on the sucker and the mother plant—with a fungicide and plant each sucker in a 3-inch pot of an equal mixture of potting soil and either vermiculite or perlite. Keep the newly planted suckers somewhat dry and in a bright place for a few weeks. Then begin regular watering.

PLANTS FROM LEAVES

Raising new plants from leaves is one of nature's great conveniences and it is fascinating to try. Select medium sized leaves, mature but not old, and remove them from the parent plant with inch-long leaf stems (petioles). The leaf stems can be placed into a glass of water or they can be planted in a half and half mixture of sand and vermiculite (expanded mica) or sand and perlite—or in ordinary gravel.

Rooting in Water

For rooting leaves in water, fill a glass with water and secure a piece of aluminum foil over the top. Make a slit in the foil and insert the leaf deep enough for its stem to be in water. Put the glass in a bright but not sunny window; roots will form in about two weeks to a month. Plant the rooted leaf stem when new plantlets are about an inch long.

You can also root leaves in water in a bowl of pebbles. Just fill the dish with small stones to support the leaf stems and keep enough water in the bowl to keep stem ends moist. In about a month a small green leaf may push out at the base of each parent leaf. When new leaves are

SEVERAL NEW PLANTS *form at base of leaf-stalk after it is inserted into porous rooting medium.*

ROOTING IN WATER *is simple and you can see the results soon. Keep leaf from touching water.*

EVEN MOISTURE in rooting mixture is assured by the pot-within-pot method. Drainage hole of smaller pot is plugged so it will hold water; this water slowly seeps through clay sides into soil.

about 1 inch long remove them (still attached to the parent leaf) and plant them in a 3-inch pot of potting soil or a mixture of vermiculite and sand.

Rooting in Soil

Another way of rooting leaves is to put them directly into an African violet potting soil or a potting soil and vermiculite mixture (about an equal percentage of each) or even vermiculite alone. The container for your rooting medium can be anything from a flower pot to a plastic or glass refrigerator container. Insert the leaf stems in the soil mixture just deep enough for them to be propped up but not so deep that they rest on it, as leaves may decay if they remain in prolonged contact with the soil. Toothpicks will help prop up heavy leaves.

At this point you have a choice of two methods: covered or uncovered. If you cover your newly-planted leaves with glass or plastic you are giving them a miniature greenhouse environment

CUT LEAF-STALKS with razor blade or very sharp knife, then insert 1/2-1 inch into rooting medium.

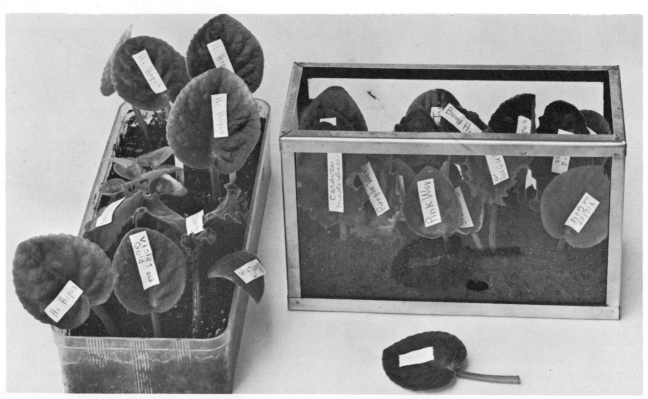

PLASTIC BOXES and aquariums are good containers for rooting African violet leaves; they conserve soil moisture, so be careful not to over-water. Tape on leaves marks variety names.

which will assure them of not drying out during the rooting period. A glass jar, a plastic bag, or the cover of a refrigerator container can be used. If you see excess moisture collecting on the sides of the covering, remove the cover for a few hours. In most cases you will not have to water the leaves under cover; natural condensation should supply enough moisture. In uncovered containers you will have to check periodically to be sure the soil does not dry out.

Place the newly-planted leaves in a bright location but out of direct sunlight. Keep the propagating mixture slightly moist but never soggy or the leaf stems may rot. About every ten days, apply a very weak solution of a soluble African violet fertilizer.

Most varieties will root and form new plants in a month to six weeks after planting the leaves; some, however, may be more stubborn to start, but as long as the leaf stays green and healthy looking, don't despair. After about five to six months plants will be ready for individual pots.

Growing from Seed

Today, fine strains of African violet seeds are sold by a number of commercial African violet growers. Although most of the seedlings you raise will not surpass (or, perhaps, even equal) the finest named varieties, the fascination of raising African violets from seed is that no two plants will be exactly alike. Raising mature plants from seed takes no longer than from leaves, but the time span from seed to blooming plant depends on the parent varieties and on the growing conditions you provide for the seedlings.

There are many soil mixtures for seed sowing that you could use, and African violet growers are continually experimenting with new formulas. Actually, if you are in a hurry, the simplest seed starting medium is vermiculite alone. Or, you can use one part milled sphagnum moss and two parts each of perlite and vermiculite. Whatever starting medium you choose, be sure that the mixture has good water holding capacity and yet is light and will drain well. Too much moisture will encourage various fungi which will rot the seeds or young seedlings; use only sterilized soil to minimize this danger.

For easy seed sowing use a shallow flowerpot (such as what is called a bulb pan) and cover it with a sheet of plastic or glass. The cover helps keep the seeds evenly moist, a condition which is essential for good germination. In preparation for seed sowing, just fill the pot with the soil mixture and gently pat it level with your hands.

Scatter the seeds lightly over the prepared soil bed in the dish or pot. Then set a sheet of glass or plastic over the seeds and put the pot in a warm (75°–80°), bright place. Germination will begin in about two weeks, although this varies somewhat depending on the parent varieties.

Keep the starting mixture barely damp but never really moist. If moisture condenses on the glass, remove the cover for a few hours. When you water, do it with a fine mist which will not disturb the soil surface and wash the seeds out of place. When you actually see green leaves poking through the medium, start watering the seedlings about once a week and using a very weak solution of a mild African violet fertilizer.

During the germination period and young seedling stage, carefully watch the new plants for any signs of damping off. This is a rot which is caused by various fungi that flourish where soil is too wet and air circulation is poor. If you see a cobwebby growth or a gray mold on the soil surface, or if the young plants begin rotting at the soil level, drench the soil with a fungicide solution (those containing Dexon are effective) or dust seedlings with captan.

When the new seedlings each have a few leaves and are about 1/2-inch tall, transplant each one into a 3-inch pot filled with a mixture of half the seed-starting medium and half your usual African violet potting soil. Try to move each plant with a tiny ball of the soil in which they have germinated clinging to their roots. Push a toothpick or nailfile into the soil below a seedling; lift it out gently, and pot each one in individual containers.

Set the newly transplanted seedlings where they will receive good light but no direct sun. After they are established they will enjoy the same amount of sunlight as mature plants do (see pages 13–14). A few weeks after transplanting (about 4–6 weeks after the seeds germinate) you can give the seedlings a weak fertilizer solution and put them on the same fertilizing schedule as your other African violets.

MAKE YOUR OWN HYBRIDS

The idea of growing your own African violets from seed is an exciting challenge because no two seedlings will be exactly alike. Directions for sowing seed and handling the seedlings you will find on page 39. At first you probably will try this with seeds you purchase from a commercial African violet grower; but once you raise a few seedlings and become fascinated by the foliage types and flower colors that appear, it is almost inevitable that you will want to make your own hybrid crosses with some particular goals in mind. If your intention is to raise seedlings which will compare favorably with new named varieties, you will have to exercise ruthless selection: Most of your seedlings will be attractive enough for you (or your friends) to grow for indoor color, but few will be really outstanding. But consider what a thrilling experience it would be if you were the first to develop a true red or yellow flower that hybridizers are seeking.

Mechanics of Hybridizing

Each African violet blossom contains the necessary male and female elements to make a cross, and these are easily seen by the naked eye. The two small yellow sacs (called *anthers*) in the center of the flower contain the dust-like pollen. The small spike that projects from the flower's center and looks like an insect's antenna is the *pistil*. The slightly enlarged tip of the pistil is the *stigma*; at the other end of the pistil (and beneath the flower) is the *ovary* which will become the seed capsule when fertilized by placing pollen on the stigma.

The best time for pollination is when the flower appears mature (although even when the flower falls off, both pollen and stigma usually are still ripe for fertilization). At this time the stigma becomes slightly sticky, enabling it to hold the pollen. To cross two flowers you must transfer the pollen from the anther of one to the stigma of another; there are several ways you can do this—it is only a matter of using whichever method seems easiest. If you cut a tiny section in an anther and let the pollen fall on your thumbnail, then you can place this pollen on a stigma of your chosen seed parent. Another simple way is to take an anther from a flower (even one that has just fallen off), slit open the pollen sac with a needle, then gently pinch the sac to open it wider and apply the opening to the sticky stigma of the seed parent. A small artists' paintbrush also can be used to transfer pollen to a stigma. During the middle of the day when the air is warm is the best time for making your crosses.

After you make a cross you may want to attach a small tag listing the names of each parent to the stem below the pollinated flower. Customarily the seed parent is listed first followed by an "X" and then the name of the pollen parent.

Within a week—if the cross is successful—you will see the seed capsule beginning to grow. As it continues to develop it will protrude more and more from the green calyx which once clasped the base of the flower. It takes anywhere from six to nine months for a seed capsule to ripen; during this time the stem beneath the developing capsule may turn or twist at an angle.

The seeds are ripe when the stem and seed capsule turn brown and start to shrivel. When this happens, remove the capsule and put it in an open dish to dry. (Small jar lids are excellent for the purpose.) Be sure to keep different crosses in separate drying dishes so the seeds will not become mixed. Set the dishes in a warm, bright spot and leave them uncovered. Many growers allow seeds to dry for about a month, but you can plant them right after harvesting or as much as a year later.

Occasionally, an apparently healthy seed capsule will turn brown and drop off long before you think it should. Don't throw it away, but instead save it and plant the seeds anyway—some of them may be fertile.

Selection

When your African violet seedlings bloom, you may discover some with colors, form, or leaf types that you would like to keep and use in additional hybridizing. Especially if you have particular goals in mind, it will pay you in terms of time and space saved to have a passing knowledge of basic genetics.

Traits are passed from generation to generation in very complex patterns. When two plants are crossed, each seed that results carries a different combination of characters derived from both parents. Some of the parent characteristics will be expressed more often in the seedlings than will other traits. Those that predominate are called *dominant*, the others are known as *recessive*. Some of the transmitted characteristics—such as flower color and leaf shape—will be easy to recognize in the seedlings; but others will be so subtle that only an experienced eye would notice them.

It is those unseen differences which often can provide the greatest excitement for you if you cross together two seedlings from the same parents. In *their* offspring—the second generation from your original cross—you may achieve the combinations of characteristics you were striving for, as the dominant and recessive traits sort themselves out to appear in arrangements that differ from their parents and grandparents.

Because most named African violet varieties are so many generations away from the wild species you often have no way of knowing what recessive characters are carried by the parent plants. For example, if you cross a white flower with a red one thinking to produce a pink-flowered seedling, you may get pink in the first generation but you are just as likely to get red, purple, white, blue, orchid, or lavender—depending upon the genetic backgrounds of the two parent plants. To achieve the pink color you wanted you might have to grow several generations of seedlings. If you are using blue-flowered and/or plain-leafed varieties in your crosses, remember that these two characters are dominant over their possible alternatives.

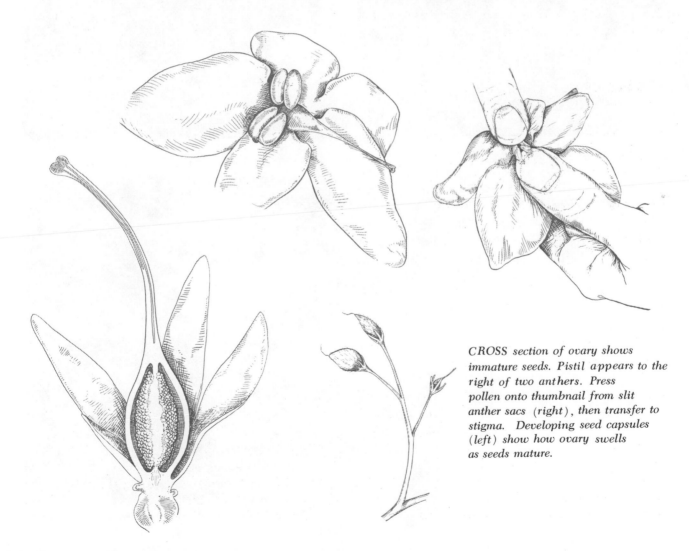

CROSS section of ovary shows immature seeds. Pistil appears to the right of two anthers. Press pollen onto thumbnail from slit anther sacs (right), then transfer to stigma. Developing seed capsules (left) show how ovary swells as seeds mature.

FAMILY PORTRAIT (top) shows an African violet and two relatives. Saintpaulia ionantha at left is followed by a Streptocarpus rexii hybrid (center) and Episcia reptans (right). Below is a spectacular hybrid gloxinia with 4-inch blossoms.

The African Violet's Colorful Cousins

WHILE THE African violet has been a household favorite for many years, there are other members of the same plant family that are, in their own distinctive ways, just as appealing for indoor and outdoor decoration. These plants are collectively referred to as "gesneriads," a term derived from the family name Gesneriaceae.

Among the gesneriads you are most likely to encounter are columnea, episcia, achimenes and gloxinia. Columneas are trailing plants grown for their brightly colored, cheerful flowers; episcias (sometimes fancifully called "flame violets"), with their tapestry-like leaves, make exotic accents even without blooms. Achimenes—either trailing or upright—are informal plants that are lavish with tubular flowers, usually in the same color range as African violets; the spectacular, often plushlike, trumpets of gloxinia flowers have made them favorite florist shop plants because of their size and sparkling clear colors. Other fine candidates where color and beauty are needed indoors are aeschynanthus, hypocyrta, kohleria, rechsteineria, smithiantha, and streptocarpus. There are also a number of seldom-seen gesneriads such as alloplectus and boea, diastema and chirita—species that are outstanding collectors' items but are not yet widely available.

All of the plants mentioned in this chapter are fine companion plants for your African violets. Generally they respond to the same kind of conditions as African violets do, although each has its own idiosyncrasies. Some of the larger of these gesneriads—aeschynanthus, columnea, kohleria—possess a virtue not shared by African violets: They can be easily used outdoors to decorate sheltered patio and porch areas.

ACHIMENES

Throughout the summer, the species and hybrids of achimenes will give you a continuous supply of cheerful, colorful flowers—a feat that seems nearly impossible when you think of the tiny rhizomes you planted only a few months earlier. Their flowers are tubular but flare out to a 5-lobed flattish face 1–3 inches across, making them look somewhat like small petunias; there are also varieties with double flowers. Colors include all the African violet shades with the addition of bright red, orange, and yellow. The plants are slender-stemmed with roundish or oval leaves of bright to dark green.

The original achimenes species came from areas of the American tropics where there is a definite alternation between wet and dry seasons. There, the plants go dormant during dry periods, beginning growth again upon return of rains. During the more than 100 years they have been in cultivation, many hybrids have been produced. These (and the parent species) fall into three general growth categories: upright (sometimes nearly to 3 feet); trailing; and fairly compact, bushy types that are intermediate between the previous two. The smaller and trailing kinds are lovely when grown to trail over the edges of a hanging basket or pot; taller sorts can be used for handsome background plantings in planters.

Rarely will you find achimenes plants available in a nursery—usually you have to start them yourself from rhizomes sold by specialty mail order suppliers. Plant them in a sterilized soil mixture that is sure to be well-drained, such as a mixture of equal parts peat moss, perlite, and leaf mold. These plants must have constant moisture during their growing season (otherwise they will go dormant) but they will not tolerate a water-logged soil.

In early spring when you receive the rhizomes, plant 5 or 6 of them to a 6-inch pot, each one about ½–1 inch beneath the soil surface. To begin growth they need a 60–70° temperature; when growth shows, move plants to a partially shaded spot and keep them well watered. Pinching out the growth tips when plants are about 3 inches tall will promote bushier growth.

When plants begin to go dormant in fall, let the soil dry out so the rhizomes will be properly cured for winter. You can leave the rhizomes in the pot (without water) over winter and resume watering in spring; or you may prefer to take them out of their soil, store them in vermiculite in a cool dry place, then repot in spring.

Here are some of the outstanding achimenes species and hybrids that you can buy from specialists. Following the name of each is a letter

TROPICAL ACHIMENES is an all-year indoor plant in cool-summer areas. Where summers are hot, move plants outdoors into areas protected from direct sunlight as soon as weather warms up.

which will tell you if the plant is compact (C), intermediate height suitable for pots or baskets (I), or tall (T).

Achimenes andrieuxii (C). A dwarf plant under 6 inches in height with bell-shaped violet and white flowers.

A. antirrhina (T). Long, slender, yellow tubes end in vivid scarlet flower faces.

A. cettoana (C). Long, narrow, dark green leaves on 10-inch, branching stems; flowers are blue.

A. flava (I). Small golden yellow blooms on rangy plants.

A. grandiflora (I). Purple flowers with white throats, sturdy stems, and attractive red-veined leaves.

A. heterophylla (I). Bright orange flowers on upright stems.

A. pedunculata (T). The tallest achimenes, with fiery orange flowers that are dotted and lined with bright red.

'Adelaide' (I). An ideal basket plant with many large, gold-throated lavender flowers.

'Atropurpurea' (C). Flowers are deep reddish-purple with lilac throats.

'Ambroise Verschaffelt' (C). A Swiss hybrid outstanding for the tracery of purple veining on the white face of the flowers.

'Camillo Brozzoni' (C). The many, small flowers are pale purple with white throats that are speckled with yellow and violet.

'Cattleya' (I). Pastel orchid-blue flowers.

'Charm' (C). Warm pink flowers on upright plants.

'Francois Cardinaux' (C). White-throated lavender flowers; profuse bloomer.

'Lady Lyttelton' (T). Red-purple flowers have prominent gold throats.

'Mme. Geheune' (I). Large red-purple flowers with red-dotted golden throats.

'Master Ingram' (T). Distinctive long orange tubes end in yellow-throated crimson flowers.

'Patens Major' (I). Flowers are very large and an

OLD FAVORITE achimenes hybrid 'Ambroise Verschaffelt' has white flowers marked purple.

intense shade of purple.

'Pulchella' (I). Numerous pale red blossoms.

'Purple King' (I). Large purple flowers have pale lavender throats minutely dotted red; very free flowering.

'Violacea Semi-Plena' (C). Deep purple, semi-double flowers on a rather dwarf plant.

'Vivid' (I). A spectacular variety for baskets, with orange-tubed magenta flowers.

COLUMNEA

All of the more than 150 columnea species are native to the tropics of Central and South America and the West Indies, where often they grow in the company of native orchids. Although some columneas are shrubby and spreading to upright, the majority of species and hybrids have relaxed, trailing stems which suit them well to growing in hanging planters. There is considerable foliage variation among the many species and hybrids—from those with tiny, buttonlike

COLUMNEA'S *trailing stems with glossy green foliage provide a polished background for the goldfish-like blooms that project outward.*

leaves to others that have large pointed leaves, either glossy or hairy—but in all cases their foliage is good-looking.

But even though the leaves are attractive, it is the brilliant flowers which make these plants really desirable: bright red, orange, yellow, and combinations of these colors. Individual blooms are tubular and as much as 3 inches long, with long, overhanging upper lobes; if you employ just a little imagination, they resemble goldfish. Some species and hybrids bloom in spring, others in summer; many of the recent hybrids flower intermittently throughout the year.

Because these are mainly epiphytic plants that often grow on trees in their native lands, a loose, gravelly soil is best for them. Add small pebbles, sand, or perlite to an African violet soil mixture to achieve a suitable loose soil structure.

Columneas will flourish in temperatures slightly cooler than you would give African violets (about 55°–60°) with a ten-degree variation between day and night readings; otherwise their culture is virtually the same.

You can start new plants from tip cuttings of young growth, using the same rooting media as described on page 38.

Many fine columnea hybrids are offered by specialty nurseries. A number of these plants originated at Cornell University, as their names often indicate. 'Campus Sunset' is yellow-flowered, each edged in red; the dark green leaves are a deep red underneath. 'Cascadilla' has large, completely red blooms and dark green foliage. 'Cayugan' has narrow leaves and orange flowers covered with red hairs. 'Cornellian' has long, narrow, glossy leaves with dark red reverses, and small yellow-orange blooms. Leaves of 'Early Bird' are light green and taper abruptly to a point; blossoms have yellow tubes and red petals. The red flowers of 'Katsura' contrast with light green and cream variegated foliage. 'Red Arrow' has large, brilliant red flowers and dark green, red-backed foliage. 'Yellow Dragon' has yellow blooms edged with red; leaves have red reverses.

EPISCIA

Colorful and often variegated foliage is the primary attraction of these plants, although the flowers are not to be ignored when plants are in bloom. Episcias are sometimes called "peacock plants" because the leaves have a metallic, iridescent sheen; these may be silver, bronze, or shades of green, frequently veined or mottled in contrasting colors. The tubular flowers have 5-lobed flat faces somewhat like achimenes; many species and hybrids are red-flowered (hence the other popular name, "flame violet"), but colors also include pink, orange, yellow, white, lavender, and spotted combinations of two colors. Flowers are borne separately rather than in clusters, intermittently throughout the year with the greatest concentration from spring through fall.

Growth habit of episcias is like that of most strawberries: They produce runners (called *stolons*), at the ends of which a small plant forms. When growing on the ground these plants will spread over a considerable area. This habit also makes them ideal hanging pot or basket subjects where they can develop into cascades of foliage.

Episcias require culture similar to that for African violets except that they prefer more water and higher humidity. Because of these differences, episcias reach their best development in greenhouses. However, they will grow satisfactorily in the home but will give you fewer flowers. Daytime temperature around 75° and no lower than 60° at night will keep plants happy.

There are many fine episcia species and named hybrids from which to choose. The following list briefly describes only some of those most widely sold.

Episcia reptans (sometimes sold as *E. fulgens*) has pebbled bronze leaves marked with willow-green veins. Red flowers.

E. cupreata. There are many varieties of this species. 'Viridifolia' has glossy green leaves with creamy veins, scarlet flowers; this has the best flowers of these *E. cupreata* varieties. 'Metallica' has olive green leaves with pale stripes and red edges. 'Chocolate Soldier' has chocolate brown, silver-veined leaves and orange-red flowers. 'Silver Sheen' has silver leaves with darker margins and light red flowers.

NOT GREEN but a rich chocolate-brown are the leaves of Episcia *'Chocolate Soldier.' Mid-rib and veins are silvery white, while blooms are bright red with yellow throats.*

PATTERNED FOLIAGE is typical of most episcias. Leaf color may be green to coppery brown.

E. dianthiflora. This is a small-leafed species, entirely green. White flowers have a distinct feathered edge and light speckles in the throats.

E. lilacina. Soft, hairy, dark bronze-green leaves are sometimes patterned with green; pale lavender flowers have yellow throats. Several hybrids between this species and *E. cupreata* have deep pink flowers: 'Pinkiscia' has large flowers and dark brownish green quilted foliage; 'Ember Lace' has white and pink variegations on its metallic green leaves.

E. melittifolia. Strong, upright-growing plant has square stems and long, narrow, glossy brown leaves with reddish undersides. Flowers are magenta.

E. punctata. Gray-green leaves and fringed creamy-white flowers spotted purple. Although not as neat a plant as *E. dianthiflora* (in a similar color) it is a better bloomer.

Still other selections offer a great variety of colors and patterns. 'Acajou' has mostly silver

leaves that are infused with dark brown from the edges, and red-orange flowers; 'Fire n' Ice' has silver leaves contrasting with bright red blooms; foliage of 'Moss Agate' is bright green with an overall netting of silver, while the large blooms are red; 'Painted Warrior' has its silver leaves tinged pink and margined with dark green (the flowers are orange-red); 'Tropical Topaz' is yellow-flowered with bright green leaves; 'Velvet Brocade' has large dark red flowers and quilted rose pink leaves margined with green.

GLOXINIA

You frequently will find flamboyant flowering plants sold in nurseries and florist shops as "gloxinias." Actually, they are just hybrids of one or more species of *Sinningia* and are discussed under that heading on page 50.

KOHLERIA

Fuzzy is the word for kohlerias. The leaves, stems, and even flower tubes are covered with short hairs that give a velvety look to the entire plant. Flowers (tubular but with flat, 5-lobed faces) are usually bright and showy; red and pink shades predominate although there are white-flowered species and a number that have purple dots contrasting with the basic flower color. The leaves may be plain green or lightly patterned in the manner of episcias. Most kohlerias can be grown either as hanging basket plants (allowing their stems to drape over the sides of a pot) or can be staked to grow upright. The species come from Mexico and northern South America.

Basic kohleria care is very similar to that for African violets: They appreciate the same soils, temperature and humidity ranges. If you can grow African violets well, then kohlerias should be easy for you, too.

Growth is produced from long, scaly rhizomes—much larger than those of achimenes. Like achimenes, however, kohlerias can go into a period of dormancy for several months, and their rhizomes should be handled in the same manner during this time. You can encourage them to grow and bloom throughout the year though, by continuing to remove old growth and by starting new plants from tip cuttings. The other propagation method is to break dormant rhizomes into 1-inch-long pieces and pot each one in a separate container.

Here are several kohleria species you may find sold by gesneriad specialists.

Kohleria amabilis is relaxed enough to be a really good hanging basket plant. The flower faces are the same bright pink as the tubes but streaked with a darker color. Leaves are soft green patterned with purplish green.

K. bogotensis has dark green foliage marked in paler green or white, often flushed with brownish red beneath. Flowers are bright red flushed and dotted yellow.

K. eriantha. The distinctive feature of this species is the red leaf-margin. Flowers are orange-red marked yellow on the 3 lower lobes.

K. lindeniana differs from the other three in having white flowers marked with violet. Leaves are veined silver and have bronze margins. Growth is compact.

RECHSTEINERIA

Although they have not achieved the popularity of these other gesneriads, rechsteinerias are nonetheless attractive and should be grown more often. The species most commonly sold form compact, broad-leafed plants that are an attractive foil for the narrowly-tubular, usually red flowers.

These are tuberous plants that need the same care as do gloxinias (see page 50). If you want to try for a year-round display from rechsteinerias, you can remove old stems that have flowered and new ones will sprout from the tuber. New plants may be started in any of several ways: by dividing the tuber, by taking leaf cuttings (as you would for African violets), and from tip cuttings.

The first species below is the one most often seen, but all three would be distinctive additions to a gesneriad collection.

Rechsteineria cardinalis. Broad, heart-shaped, fuzzy leaves grow in opposite pairs on the stems

to form a compact plant. Against these appear the brilliant red, 2-inch-long flowers; bloom is in summer, but you can have plants flowering at Christmas if you start tubers in the fall.

R. leucotricha also is known by its common name, Brazilian edelweiss. In this species, silvery leaves are covered with white hairs, against which the salmon-red flowers show off handsomely.

R. verticillata is popularly known as the "umbrella plant" because it produces whorls of leaves which appear to encircle the stems, thus producing an umbrella effect. Purple-spotted pink flowers appear in clusters above the topmost whorl of leaves.

VELVETY FLOWERS *and leaves characterize* Kohleria amabilis. *Both are marked with purple.*

SINNINGIA

Two distinctly different types of plants are included in this genus. The first and most notable is the spectacular florists' gloxinia; second come the other species sinningias which are less flashy but no less worthwhile in a gesneriad collection. Basic culture is stated in the next section on gloxinias—any differences for the species will be noted in their descriptions.

Gloxinias

Next to African violets, the gloxinia is the most popular house plant among the gesneriads. In fact, none of the various gesneriads can match gloxinias for size and impact of the individual flowers. These are wide, flaring, bell-shaped tubes—sometimes as much as four inches across—in white, lavender, pink, red, purple, dark maroon, and various combinations of the colors with white in the throat, on the edges, or as a background for colored speckles. Most of these flowers face upward so you can look directly into them. Foliage is in proportion to the flowers and matches them in magnificence: rich velvety green and broadly oval.

This type of gloxinia arose by chance during the nineteenth century from seedlings of *Sinningia speciosa, S. maxima,* or possibly from each one. Before that time, all gloxinias had nodding flowers rather than the upward-facing ones which these seedlings exhibited. Because the first to flower was raised by a Scottish gardener, John Fyfe, the type was known as 'Fyfiana'—a name which is sometimes still attached to these varieties.

Gloxinias grow from tubers and they naturally go through a dormant period each year when all growth dies back. When a healthy plant produces no more leaves or flower buds, this is your signal that the dormant stage is approaching. Gradually withhold water until the leaves yellow, then stop watering so they will dry out. From 1½-3 months the tubers will lie dormant and will need only enough moisture to keep them plump—usually just enough to prevent the soil from drying out completely. Storage temperature should be around 60°. Often new growth will begin which will signal the end of dormancy, but if, after three months, none has appeared, assume the tuber is ready to resume growth.

Pot new tubers—or repot old ones—in a soil mixture that is well-drained and rich. Add sand to prepared African violet soil (about 3 parts mix to one part sand) or prepare one using the materials and proportions shown on page 19. Place the tuber about 1 inch below the surface of the soil and be sure the indented top side of the tuber faces up. Water moderately until roots are established; thereafter give plants generous waterings but allow the soil *surface* to dry out between waterings. If you see, later in the season, that roots have filled the container, shift the plant into the next larger sized pot.

Originally from the South American tropics, gloxinias prefer a fairly warm nighttime temperature—around 65°—and daytime temperatures in the low 70's. They don't demand excessively high humidity (about 50% is adequate), but if your home atmosphere is on the dry side you should provide for extra humidity in their growing area. One of the simplest methods is to fill a tray with gravel, set the potted plants on the gravel surface, then add water to the gravel. The water will continually evaporate from the gravel and increase humidity in the immediate area, but soil won't become water-logged because the pots do not sit in the water.

Protect gloxinias from hot summer sun, but otherwise see that they receive plenty of light and even some direct sunlight during spring and fall. Well-lighted locations promote compact growth; too little will give you sparse, leggy plants.

The same fertilizing program as suggested on page 16 for African violets will also be appreciated by your gloxinias.

You can grow new gloxinia plants using any one of four propagating techniques as well as from seed. Large, old tubers can be cut into two or more pieces as long as each piece contains at least one growth eye. Dust the cut surfaces with a fungicide to prevent rot. Older tubers usually send up more than one stem; if you allow all stems to develop to the point where each has at least two sets of leaves you can remove all but one and root them under cover of glass or plastic. Leaf cuttings can be done two ways: The direc-

BOLD BLOSSOMS of hybrid gloxinias (sinningias) may be rich and velvety or delicately speckled and ruffled. Large, rugged leaves are equally impressive.

tions on page 38 for rooting African violet leaf-cuttings also apply to gloxinias. And in addition to this, you can remove a healthy (but not the largest) leaf from your plant, cut its main ribs in several places on the leaf underside, then insert the leaf-stem in the rooting medium and lay the leaf on the soil so that the cut veins are in contact with it. Under cover of glass or plastic, new tubers will develop at the leaf-stem and wherever cuts in the veins were made. When the leaf dies, pot all new tubers separately in 3-inch pots.

Sinningia Species

These species are not as widely available as their flashier gloxinia relatives, and because of this they are seen much less often. They are, however, just as attractive in a more unassuming manner. Grow these plants just as you would gloxinias.

Sinningia barbata has small (to 1½ inches long) white flowers in which the narrow tube has expanded into a bladder-like pouch. Leaves are about 6 inches long, deep bluish-green and prom-inently veined; the undersides are red-purple. Growth is shrubby to about 12 inches.

S. eumorpha flowers differ from those of the previous species in having only a slightly swollen (rather than bladder-like) tube; these, too, are white marked with red in the throats. Although the green, 4-inch leaves appear glossy, they are covered with small white hairs; undersides are lighter green and stems are reddish.

S. regina is the closest in appearance of these species to gloxinias, but the silver-veined leaves with their red undersides are a distinguishing feature. Flowers are borne singly on stems that rise about six inches above the leaves; the nodding, trumpet shaped flowers are violet with lighter, speckled throats and are about two inches long.

S. tubiflora is the tallest plant of this group, sometimes reaching four feet. Leaves are oblong, green and hairy, to about five inches. Although it may be reluctant to flower unless grown in strong light, it will bear fragrant tubular white flowers—each about four inches long in one-sided groups at the ends of stems.

SMITHIANTHA

The common name for these plants is "temple bells" and describes well the character of the flowers. They come in quite a wide range of colors and color combinations, carried face down (like bells) in flower spikes at the ends of stems which may reach two feet high. Leaves usually are heart-shaped and so densely hairy that they have the look of velvet.

The species are native to the mountains of Mexico and neighboring Guatemala where they enjoy somewhat cool temperatures and moderate to high humidity. In cultivation, they need the same treatment as achimenes (see page 44). Smithianthas grow from scaly rhizomes as do achimenes, but in this case the rhizomes are large and should be planted one to a container. You can propagate them by breaking up the rhizomes into smaller pieces at planting time or by taking leaf cuttings (as you would for African violets) during the growing season.

Recently, a series of fine smithiantha hybrids has come from Cornell University; these range in color from warm pastels through red. These are robust, showy plants with either red leaves (the named selections 'Capistrano,' 'Carmel,' 'San Gabriel,' and 'Santa Clara') or green leaves ('Abbey,' 'Cathedral,' 'Cloister,' and 'Vespers'). More easily, however, you may find plants or rhizomes available of the following species, sometimes incorrectly labeled *Naegelia*.

Smithiantha cinnabarina is a striking plant with velvety red hairs on green leaves, making leaves appear solid red to red-brown. Flowers are brick red.

S. multiflora has velvety green leaves that are distinctly lighter underneath. Flowers may be either cream or white.

S. zebrina is marked with brown or purple along the leaf-veins, giving rise to the specific name *zebrina*. Flowers are scarlet with red-spotted yellow throats.

PLUSH-LIKE bronzy leaves of Smithiantha cinnabarina *complement the brilliant red-orange blooms.*

BELL-SHAPED, down-facing flowers on smithiantha illustrate common name, "temple bells."

OTHER GESNERIADS

There are many other gesneriads which can be attractive and satisfactory house plants. Any relative lack of popularity is due to lack of availability. If you do find a nursery or mail order catalog which carries additional gesneriads, chances are that they will be from among these three: aeschynanthus, hypocyrta, and streptocarpus.

Aeschynanthus

You may find plants of aeschynanthus masquerading under the incorrect name *trichosporum*. The species are native to Southeast Asia and might be considered the Old World counterpart of the tropical American columneas. Their trailing growth is well suited to hanging baskets, from which you can see easily their brilliant tubular flowers and (in some species) attractively mottled foliage. Aeschynanthus prefers higher temperature, humidity, and more light than most other gesneriads; its best development usually is in greenhouses. *Aeschynanthus lobbianus* has 2-inch tubular red flowers which account for its common name "lipstick vine"; *A. marmoratus* is grown chiefly for its green leaves mottled maroon rather than for its green flowers; *A. speciosus* has bright yellow and orange flowers up to four inches long.

Hypocyrta

In appearance and culture hypocyrta is closest to columnea, and like columnea is native to tropical America. Flowers of most species are orange (although there are red and yellow sorts) and are noticeably pouch-shaped. Given the warmth and humidity they really prefer, they tend to be nearly everblooming. Swollen joints that occur on older growth will root easily if they come in contact with soil; new plants also grow from tip cuttings.

Hypocyrta nummularia has small, shiny leaves on trailing stems; flowers are red-orange.

H. selloana grows stiffly erect and has large, pointed leaves; flowers are brick red with the pouch on the upper part of the bloom.

FOR WARM CLIMATES and greenhouses anywhere, aeschynanthus offers trailing stems, bright blooms.

H. radicans is also trailing and small-leafed but thick-textured and dark green with large, bright orange blooms.

Streptocarpus

"Cape primrose" is the name applied to many of these plants, referring to the primrose-like appearance of some species and to the homeland of the first species discovered—South Africa, once generally called the Cape of Good Hope or simply "the Cape." Subsequent discoveries revealed that streptocarpus species vary considerably in sizes and shapes of leaves and flowers and in growth habit, including some species that have but a single leaf per plant.

Flowering season on mature plants of the most familiar hybrids is autumn and winter. But because many will grow to blooming size within four to six months from the sowing of seed, you can have plants blooming almost throughout the year. Many of the species and their hybrids are perennials which can be increased by dividing the multiple crowns (as you would African violets) after the blooming period to perpetuate favorite ones.

MINIATURE GESNERIADS

African violets have no corner on the miniatures market. Many of the other gesneriads described in this chapter also have scaled-down versions which can be enjoyed individually for their diminutive beauty or as components of miniature landscapes.

These miniatures definitely are happier in the humid, more even-tempered atmosphere of a terrarium or other glass garden. Even soil moisture is especially important for the tiny gesneriads that grow from rhizomes; if plants get too dry they go into dormancy and it is difficult to get them growing well again.

Among hybrids between sinningia and rechsteineria (called Gloxinera) are a number of miniatures. Gloxinera 'Cupid Doll' has medium green leaves with red veins and purple tubular flowers; 'Pink Petite' has tiny pale green, hairy leaves and salmon pink trumpet flowers; 'Ramadeva' has violet-throated pink blooms. Miniature sinningia hybrids include: 'Dollbaby' with lilac and white flowers; 'Tom Thumb' with white-bordered red blooms; and 'Wood Nymph'— purple flowers, spotted in the throat. *Streptocarpus kirkii* has rosettes of rounded leaves and lavender to purple trumpet-like blossoms.

Streptocarpus kirkii

LIPSTICK-LIKE tubes that surround flowers of aeschynanthus coupled with orange to red blooms show why popular name is "lipstick vine."

A temperature range slightly cooler than you would give African violets (about 55°–60°) and plenty of light without direct sunlight will be successful for these plants. Soil mixtures that are suitable for African violets also will be satisfactory for streptocarpus. In addition to raising plants from seed and division, new plants may be started from leaf cuttings. This can be done either by inserting the leaf stem in a rooting medium (see page 38) or by laying the leaf down on the rooting medium so that new plants will form along the principal leaf veins.

Streptocarpus rexii hybrids are the most widely available. These have long, wavy, stemless leaves which in time form clumps of foliage. Flowers are trumpet-shaped, to three inches long and two inches across, in white, pink, purple, red, and blue—often marked with a contrasting color in their throats.

S. saxorum has inch-long, very hairy leaves on trailing stems which drape well from hanging baskets. Its white-throated lavender flowers are trumpet-shaped and are borne at the ends of pendant flower stalks.

PRIMROSE-LIKE growth habit and flowers are easy to recognize in this Streptocarpus rexii *hybrid.*

DELICATE HYBRID streptocarpus 'Constant Nymph' has yellow-throated lavender blossoms about 1 inch across, and narrow, dark green leaves.

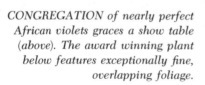

CONGREGATION of nearly perfect
African violets graces a show table
(above). The award winning plant
below features exceptionally fine,
overlapping foliage.

FIRST
PLACE

Grooming and Showing Your African Violets

T O ANYONE who becomes fascinated with African violets there comes a time when he will want to attend an African violet show. There, under one roof, can be observed countless varieties that have been groomed and preened to present the best appearance possible for each plant. This allows the showgoer to make reasonably accurate comparative evaluations of the varieties on exhibit. But while viewing the plants, comparing varieties, and generally soaking up the beauty of all those nearly flawless specimens, you are likely to respond to a powerful but unspoken challenge: to try to develop some of your own African violets into show plants. It is difficult to describe the immense satisfaction of producing a specimen worthy of entering in a show—even if your plant doesn't come away with an award ribbon.

The spirit of friendly competition generated by a show does more than just bring forth displays of superbly grown plants. Perhaps more important is that shows bring together fellow hobbyists where they can share experiences and see new developments; and they invariably lure newcomers into the ranks of African violet growing.

If you decide you want to try exhibiting your own African violet plants, find out the dates of the next show you could enter. This will let you know exactly how much time you have to get your plants into first class show condition. The points on which a plant is judged are listed on page 58. Remember that, even though your potential show specimens may fall short of perfection, there are some "tricks of the trade" you can employ in the weeks before show time to correct what would be judged as faults. See page 60 for these, and start working on your plants as soon as you know when the next show will be held.

It also is a good idea to obtain a copy of the schedule of the show you want to enter. This will list all the classes in which plants may be entered, including group entry categories and any special classes not included in a standard schedule like

WELL-BALANCED show specimen of African violet 'Wintergreen' has nearly perfect rosette of unblemished leaves (newer leaves are variegated) and abundant flowers.

the one shown on page 59. At the same time, carefully read the show rules which will be clearly stated in the schedule. These explain such things as time and place to enter your plants, and what awards are being offered.

THE MAKING OF A SHOW PLANT

In order to produce a specimen African violet that has a chance of competing successfully in a show, you will need to know what qualities of a plant are judged and how important each one is in the overall evaluation. Five aspects of a plant are considered in the judging, and each of the five has a maximum number of points assigned to it. When added together the points total 100—which would indicate a perfect show specimen.

The basic ribbons awarded at shows are for first, second, and third places, and honorable mention. The awarding of these is determined by the total number of points a plant scores dur-

ing the judging. For a blue (first place) ribbon a plant needs 90–100 points; second place (red ribbon) plants must score 80–89 points; white (third place) ribbons go to specimens in the 70–79 point range; to receive honorable mention a plant needs 65–69 points.

Here is the point scale used by the African Violet Society of America and which will be used in all shows held under their rules. Shows that are held according to rules of the American Gesneria Society or Saintpaulia International will employ a slightly different point scale for these categories.

Plant form (30 points). Plant symmetry is what the judges will look for first. A perfectly symmetrical plant will have its leaves distributed evenly in a circle—like the spokes of a bicycle wheel arising from the plant's center. This is the most difficult quality to perfect since you often have to train your plants carefully (and handle them even more carefully) to achieve a perfectly even distribution of leaves. Not all African violets can conform to one standard in this category—some

SAMPLE SHOW SCHEDULE

Although not all African violet shows will offer all these categories (and some shows may have additional specialty classes), this is a representative "complete" schedule which allows for all possible flower colors and forms.

SECTION 1

Single blossom specimen plants, standard types
Class: 1. Pinks
2. Whites
3. Orchids and lavenders
4. Purples and dark blues
5. Medium and light blues
6. Reds and wines
7. Bi-colors, multicolors, Genevas, variegated blossoms

SECTION 2

Double blossom specimen plants, standard types
Class: 8. Pinks
9. Whites
10. Orchids and lavenders
11. Purples and dark blues
12. Medium and light blues
13. Reds and wines
14. Bi-colors, multicolors, Genevas, variegated blossoms

SECTION 3

Single blossom specimen plants, Supreme types
Class: 15. Pinks
16. Whites
17. Orchids and reds
18. Purples and blues
19. Bi-colors, multicolors, Genevas, variegated blossoms

SECTION 4

Double blossom specimen plants, Supreme types
Class: 20. Pinks
21. Whites
22. Orchids and reds
23. Purples and blues
24. Bi-colors, multicolors, Genevas, variegated blossoms

SECTION 5

All specimen plants with variegated foliage, single and double blossoms, standard and Supreme types
Class: 25. Pinks
26. Whites
27. Orchids and lavenders
28. Purples and dark blues
29. Medium and light blues
30. Reds and wines
31. Bi-colors, multicolors, Genevas, variegated blossoms

SECTION 6

Miniature and semi-miniature specimen plants, single and double blossoms, green and variegated foliage
Class: 32. Pinks
33. Whites
34. Orchids and lavenders
35. Purples and dark blues
36. Medium and dark blues
37. Reds and wines
38. Bi-colors, multicolors, Genevas, variegated blossoms

SECTION 7

Original Armacost & Royston hybrids
Class: 39. One plant of each of the ten original hybrids (see page 6 for list of these); each plant must score 85 points or more.

SECTION 8

Seedlings and mutations
Class: 40. Mutations and sports
41. Seedlings

SECTION 9

Specimen plants of species and trailing types
Class: 42. African violet species
43. Trailing hybrids

SECTION 10

Specimen gesneriad plants other than African violets
Class: 44. Columnea
45. Episcia
46. Gloxinia
47. Any other gesneriad
48. Miniature gesneriads

SECTION 11

Terrariums
Class: 49. Gardens under glass, featuring all live plants with African violets predominating and in bloom

are naturally more compact than others, some naturally grow flat while others may tend to present a more rounded outline because newer leaves grow upward at an angle from the plant's crown—but the even spacing of leaves should be possible even though growth habits vary from variety to variety.

Quantity of bloom (25 points). Although plentiful bloom is the objective, it is not always the plant with the most flowers that will score the most points. Rather, the amount of bloom is judged according to variety—some are less free-flowering than others and so have to be scored according to the amount of bloom normal for the variety. The 'Supreme' varieties, for example, typically produce fewer flowers than many other kinds but compensate by having larger-than-normal blooms.

Cultural perfection (20 points). A perfectly symmetrical specimen smothered in flowers still can fail to make it to the award table if it shows evidence of careless culture or grooming. Except for varieties with naturally variegated foliage, leaves should be evenly green. Any brown, dead leaf edges, sunbleached or insect damaged leaves will take away points. Poor grooming also will do the same, as points will be deducted for dusty or dead leaves, dead flowers, and visible insects.

Size of blooms (15 points). The judges follow the same guidelines here as they do when evaluating the amount of bloom: Some varieties naturally produce larger flowers than others. Therefore, bloom size is judged according to what size flower a variety is expected to produce.

Color of blooms (10 points). Cultural conditions—such as the amount and intensity of light a plant receives, the soil it grows in, the quality of water you give to it—all influence somewhat the color of flowers. Not that differences in conditions will give you white flowers instead of pink. But the intensity of colors can vary, so that a plant of a particular variety that is showing washed-out color will not score as highly as a plant of the same variety which exhibits blooms of a more "normal" shade.

Training and Grooming

The most important training methods are those which are directed toward making a plant symmetrical. Ideally, this training should begin when the plant is small, so that your training more often will be guidance rather than correction.

Begin by placing the young plant exactly in the center of its pot; a symmetrical specimen that is growing off-center in its container will lose points at judging time. Then, be sure to turn the plant frequently—as often as once a day would not be too much, but once a week should be the absolute minimum. Turning insures that all leaves on all sides of the plant receive approximately equal light, preventing a tendency to grow lopsided which happens if one side of a plant is more constantly exposed to light than is the other.

If, as the leaves grow out, they become unevenly spaced, or if you should accidentally break off a leaf, you still can restore even spacing. Place toothpicks or other small sticks into the soil and against the leaf stalk on the side *away* from the gap you are trying to fill. Gradually move the position of the picks toward the gap—the leaves will adjust to each new position after a few days.

CLOSE GAP between leaves by shifting leaves closer together using toothpicks as guides.

To achieve absolutely equal spacing you sometimes may have to shift each leaf's position slightly; always it is the leaves on either side of the gap which will need the most shifting.

Another symmetry problem arises when a leaf or two fail to lie in the same plane as the others in the rosette. When you encounter one of these individualists that sticks out above the rest of the leaves, bring it back into line by looping a hairpin or bent piece of wire over the leaf stalk and inserting the ends into the soil so that the leaf is pulled down into position. After a while you can remove the wire and the leaf will stay in place.

Unless you plan to encourage multiple crowned plants for entry in those show classifications, you will want to watch for and remove any suckers that start to develop. Carefully pinch or break off suckers before they grow so large that they begin to interfere with the plant's symmetry. **Grooming** is the easiest phase of preparing a plant for showing, but in the excitement (and, often, haste) that precedes show entry it is the phase easiest to neglect. Assuming that your African violet show entry is a well-balanced plant, that it has a good amount of bloom for the variety, and that the container is neither too small nor too large for the plant's size, then you should check these details:

- Is the pot clean?
- Are the leaves free of dust?
- Are there any visible insects?
- Are all dead or dying leaves and flowers removed?
- Have you removed any leaves or flowers that show disease or insect damage?
- Have you removed all training aids (toothpicks, wire)?
- Is there a tag on the plant which tells its varietal name?
- Is your name attached to the plant so that no mixup can occur following the show?

An artist's paintbrush can be one of your greatest grooming aids. Use it to whisk away dust, soil particles on leaves, and insects. To keep your name with your plant, one of the easiest methods involves only an ordinary pencil (whose writing will not smear or vanish if it gets wet) and an adhesive tape. Write your name on the tape and attach the tape to the bottom of the plant's pot.

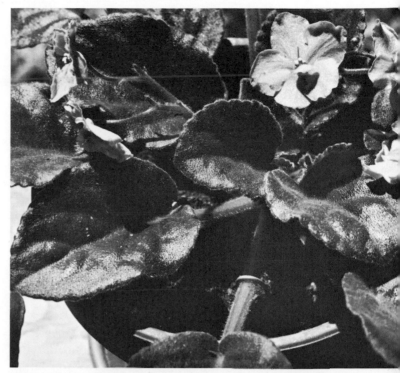

WIRE LOOP, hooked around leaf-stalk and inserted into soil, will pull leaf down into position.

IDENTIFY PLANT (and its ownership) by applying adhesive tape marker to bottom of dry pot.

GETTING IT THERE—IN ONE PIECE

Your weeks or months of loving care and careful training are only time wasted if you cannot safely transport your African violets to the show site. What could be more heartbreaking than the perfect symmetry of a plant ruined by the breakage of one or more leaves when you had to make a quick stop or sudden turn on your way to the show? What you need, then, is a transporting device in which your plants will stand upright, always remain apart from one another, and will not be damaged even if the carrier should slide around.

While there are probably many ways in which you could get plants to a show undamaged, there is one time-tested method which bears repeating because it is simple and uses materials available to almost everyone. All you need are two cardboard boxes (one several inches smaller than the other in length and width) and some newspaper.

Let's assume you have two show plants that you have to transport by car. First, take the smaller cardboard carton and cut the sides down to slightly less than the height of the pots; then cut two holes in the box bottom that will be the diameter of the pots and far enough apart so that the plants' leaves won't touch when the plants are placed in the holes. When you turn the carton upside down and slip the pots into the holes, the pot rims should just fit so that the pots are held securely in place.

For transport to a show, put the smaller box (with the holes) upside-down into the larger box and stuff the spaces between the two with newspaper. Then, set your African violets into the holes; their leaves should not touch each other (if you cut the holes far enough apart) and they should not touch the sides of the larger box. Now, as long as the box remains on a flat surface (like the floor of your car) throughout its journey to the show, it can slide around without damage to the plants.

CONVENIENT CARRIER for show plants is made from two cardboard boxes, one with cutouts to hold pots.

INVERT smaller box into larger, stuff gaps between with newspaper, then set in plants.

SIMPLE COMPOSITION and economy of materials that are all in scale with one another produce attractive arrangement. Leaves used with African violet flowers are Maidenhair fern.

FLOWER ARRANGEMENT WITH AFRICAN VIOLETS

A happy by-product of growing African violets—and one that is frequently overlooked—is their provision of flowers for arrangements. Just a small bouquet of African violets alone in a small vase of water can be surprisingly attractive. Don't hesitate to pick the flowers, as picking does no harm to the plant.

When you work with African violets in arrangements that include other materials, keep in mind how small their flowers are. In larger arrangements, especially, they are best used as decorative fill-in material rather than as the star performers. If you use branches, driftwood, or stones in your arrangement, African violet flowers can be tucked in at the base of these materials to suggest a natural planting.

Miniature arrangements are, of course, where African violets can shine as the solo artists with no other flowers for competition. However, their blooms also are undeniably suited for use in arrangements with other miniature flowers (such as daffodils and tulips), grassy foliage, and small seed pods.

Most African violet shows have categories for flower arrangements that feature African violets. Arrangement judging, according to African Violet Society of America rules, also is done by a point system.

Design of the entire flower arrangement may receive a maximum of 30 points; 25 points are possible for the best *use of color*; up to 20 points may be given for *distinction and originality* of the arrangement; *suitability of materials* (whether or not they go well together and are in pleasing scale to the African violet flowers) counts for 15 points; finally 10 points are at stake for the *condition* (freshness and lack of damage to flowers and leaves) of the total arrangement.

Classes in which entire African violet plants are used in an "arrangement" (such as in terrariums, miniature landscapes, and dish gardens) are judged by the same point system as are arrangements. Here, the symmetry and condition of the plant are considered under the 10-point category *condition*. However, these plants are evaluated according to their overall effect in the arrangement composition rather than as horticultural specimens.

African Violet Shopping Guide

Many people get their first African violets from florist shops or from the houseplant section of a supermarket. When you have a chance like this to personally select plants, take the time to study them carefully before making a purchase. Look for individuals that have fresh, perky leaves and in a symmetrical arrangement if it is a single-crown plant. Avoid plants that have spotted, stained, or otherwise discolored leaves. These may indicate pests at work, but even if not it means your plant will be less than beautiful until healthy new leaves grow out and mature. As a final check, don't forget to pick up the plant and look at the undersides of the leaves to be sure they are free from insects.

If you are just starting out with African violets, here are a few suggestions. Start out with the varieties that have plain green leaves; they are generally easier to grow than some of the fancy frilled-leaf sorts. This implies no sacrifice of flower beauty, though—you'll find the complete range of colors and color combinations, both single and double, in plain-leafed hybrids. If light presents a problem, remember that the varieties with pale green leaves and silvery undersides usually require less light than the dark green leafed sorts and those with red leaf backs.

Once you have grown a few African violets and discovered the ideal growing environment for them, you probably will want to add some of the newer and fancier varieties to your collection. The easiest way to get these is to select them from catalogues of mail-order African violet specialists. When you buy African violets through catalogues, you have no chance to select personally the individual plants. Fortunately, most suppliers are reputable and will ship only healthy, thriving plants such as you would pick out if you could.

If plants you order by mail look somewhat wilted upon arrival, don't become alarmed; this is not uncommon, and plants should completely revive within a few days. Put the new plants in a light but not sunny place and water them only moderately until they show, by their generally healthy appearance, that they have adjusted to the new environment.

WHITE

Agnew. Double white blooms and tailored foliage.

Avalon White. Large semi-double white star flowers. Dark, tailored foliage.

Blizzard Supreme. Large white double blooms. Supreme type foliage.

Breckinridge. Plain foliage and double white flowers.

Bronze N'White. Dark bronzy leaves, white double blooms.

Butterfly White. Dark, heart-shaped leaves. Double white flowers.

Buttermilk. Double blossoms are creamy white. Dark, slightly fluted, red-backed foliage.

Crystal. Semi-double white star flowers. Green, tailored foliage.

Dixie Snow. White double blooms open green, then fade to white. Foliage is wavy and flat.

Emogene Sport. Plain foliage and white double flowers.

Frosted Snow Prince. Flowers are single white. Variegated foliage.

Honey Bunny. White semi-double blooms. Tailored foliage.

Ivory Buttons. Double ivory white blossoms. Pink and green spooned foliage.

Missouri Cloud Cliff. Frilled white star flowers. Girl foliage.

Moon Drops. Blooms are semi-double, fluted white. Ruffled, apple green foliage.

Orion. Double white blooms and plain foliage.

Pearl Moon. Round, serrated leaves. White single star flowers.

Puff Ball. Large pure white double flowers. Light green, tailored foliage.

Pure Innocence. Wavy leaves and double fringed white blossoms.

Snow. Large double white blooms. Plain green leaves.

Tommie Lou. Double white flowers. Leaves are variegated and tailored.

Westdale Summer Snow. Double white blooms. Quilted foliage on a large plant.

Westwind's Sweet Sugar. Slightly pointed, tailored foliage that is sometimes ruffled. Frilly pure white double blooms.

White Cockade. Dark, glossy leaves. White flowers are double.

White Cup. Greenish white double blooms. Small, tailored foliage.

White Tango. Large flowers are double white. Grotei foliage.

White Sayles. Fringed leaves and double white blooms.

MEDIUM AND LIGHT BLUE

Attention. Tailored leaves. Light blue single blooms.

Azure Skies. Large star flowers of light, bright blue. Medium green, spooned foliage.

Bit of Heaven. Plain green foliage. Light blue double flowers.

Blue Excitement. Quilted leaves and medium blue double blooms.

Blue Falcon. Double wisteria blue. Quilted, dark green foliage.

Blue Hawaii. Large medium blue double. Tailored foliage on a large plant.

Bluejean. Nearly single medium blue with extra small center petal. Quilted, scalloped foliage.

Blue Max. Dark leaves and medium blue double flowers.

Blue Mirror. Shiny, almost black leaves. Blue double flowers.

Blue Reverie. Sky blue single blooms. Both foliage and flowers are frilled.

Blue Rosette. Double medium blue blooms. Plain foliage.

Blue Skies of Aurora. Semi-double royal blue. Quilted, pointed foliage. Grows large.

Blue Yonder. Tailored leaves. Flowers are light blue doubles.

Bluzette. Frilly leaves. Frilled medium blue double blooms.

Boutique. Double, pale powder blue. Small, tailored foliage.

Brenda. Ruffled, variegated leaves. Flowers are frilled single blue Genevas.

Cheer Up. Soft foliage. Blue semi-double star Geneva flowers.

Cisco. Wavy powder blue double flowers. Dark longifolia leaves. Grows large.

Cool Shadows. Bright blue double flowers. Tailored foliage.

Cupid's Bow. Tailored, flat-growing foliage. Double frilled blue flowers.

Darling Blue. Light blue semi-double blooms. Dark, slightly ruffled foliage.

Dorothy Young. Quilted leaves. Flowers are medium blue and double.

Elsie. Pointed, serrated leaves. Medium blue double blooms.

Fringed Wedgewood. Dark, frilled leaves. Frilled light blue double flowers.

Gay Pioneer. Double blue flowers and plain foliage. Grows large.

Gay Song. Wavy leaves. Fringed blue double blooms.

Gentian. Tailored leaves. Double blue star flowers.

Grand Parade. Very dark, quilted, red-backed leaves. Semi-double blue blooms.

Hoodwink. Standard foliage. Medium blue Geneva blooms.

Hooterville. Dark, pointed, quilted leaves. Flowers are powder blue and semi-double.

Kenya Violet. Shiny leaves and double blue blooms.

Mara. Dark, frilled leaves. Frilled bright blue double flowers.

Mighty Mini. Large powder blue star blooms. Dark green, slightly notched, quilted foliage.

Mighty Nice. Semi-double, medium blue star flowers. Heart-shaped, medium green, notched foliage.

Mini Skirt. Extra double and large powder blue blooms. Small, neat foliage. Extra small grower.

Monterey. Trailing, basket type plant. Medium blue double flowers and round, dark green foliage.

Morning Sky. Tailored leaves. Flowers are blue and double.

Pacific Lagoon. Red-backed leaves. Flowers are single Geneva stars.

Quiet Waters. Tailored leaves and blue double blooms.

Rhapsodie Ruth. Plain green foliage. Single blue flowers.

R. K. Pacemaker. Tailored leaves. Double blue Geneva blooms.

Shine Boy. Slick, shiny foliage. Small, medium blue, semi-double blossoms.

Ski Trails. Plain green foliage. Medium blue, single Geneva flowers.

Timber Top. Tailored leaves. Powder blue double flowers.

Top Flight. Tailored leaves and double blue blooms.

Tricksy Blue. Glossy leaves. Light blue star flowers.

U. C. Matchless. Tailored leaves. Double sky blue Geneva blooms.

Val's Big Beauty. Tailored, variegated leaves. Medium blue double flowers.

Vibrant Blue. Bright dark blue blooms. Light green foliage.

Violet Carey. Semi-double blue-violet flowers. Medium sized, dainty grower with dark foliage.

Voyageur. Large, fluted, full light blue double.

Wallington. Compact grower with dark foliage. Flowers are bright blue and semi-double.

Wanda. Dark leaves. Pale blue double flowers.

Westdale Blue Dale. Semi-double blue flowers and strawberry foliage.

Westdale Velvet. Standard foliage. Single blue Geneva flowers.

Windermere. Large light medium blue, loosely double. Flat, quilted, pointed foliage.

DARK BLUE AND PURPLE

After Dark. Large deep purple, semi-double blooms. Tailored leaves.

After Five. Wavy, variegated leaves and ruffled deep purple single flowers.

Baby Girl. Double midnight purple bloom. Variegated foliage. Grows large.

Beau Prince. Dark ruffled leaves. Flowers are fringed double purple Genevas.

Big One. Single purple bloom. Dark, red-backed foliage. Grows large.

Billie Blue. Tailored leaves. Deep blue double flowers.

Blossom Time. Huge, ruffled, royal blue double flowers. Wavy leaves.

Blue Cadet. Compact, tailored leaves. Deep blue tufted star flowers.

Blue Onyx. Plain green foliage. Dark purple double blooms.

Bonnie Blue. Tailored leaves and deep blue double flowers.

Charades. Double dark blue blooms. Spooned, glossy foliage.

Charlemagne. Flowers are large deep purple doubles. Round, soft leaves.

Checkmate. Tailored leaves. Double purple Geneva flowers.

Cheerful Chap. Slightly wavy leaves. Dark purple double blooms.

Clematis. Single purple star blooms. Medium green, quilted leaves. Grows large.

Close Up. Flowers are purple singles. Dark, quilted foliage.

Curtis G. Scalloped, quilted, round foliage. Single deep pansy purple blooms.

Dapper Dan. Dark blue double flowers and plain foliage.

Dark Horizon. Tailored leaves. Dark blue single Geneva blooms.

Dawn Purple. Plain green leaves with red backs. Blooms are plum purple and double.

Dean. Double, dark, blue-purple blooms. Quilted foliage.

Deep Purple. Quilted leaves have a tendency to spoon. Double violet blossoms.

French Knight. Fringed purple star flowers. Black-green, wavy foliage.

Ginger. Quilted leaves and double purple blooms.

Glitter Gulch. Dark, quilted, red-backed leaves. Wavy purple star flowers.

Go Light. Tailored leaves. Blooms are velvety purple, semi-double Genevas.

Guardsman. Dark, wavy leaves and dark blue double flowers.

Gypsy Wildcat. Quilted leaves. Flowers are large purple doubles.

Indigo Maid. Double purple blooms. Tailored foliage.

Jimmy John. Tiny, tailored leaves. Dark blue single flowers.

Leigh. Fringed, dark blue-purple flowers and tailored foliage.

Linda Blue. Quilted, ruffled leaves. Blue-violet double Geneva blooms.

Look Smart. Double dull blue star flowers. Dark tailored foliage.

Majenta Pirate. Dark leaves. Blooms are frilled purple and single.

Marine Blue. Quilted leaves. Deep blue double star flowers.

Memories. Huge purple single flowers with tailored foliage.

Midnight Magic. Quilted ruffled leaves. Dark blue double blooms.

Missouri Starry Night. Tailored foliage. Very dark blue star flowers.

Neca Chief. Semi-double, dark blue Geneva blooms. Tailored, flexible foliage.

Night Rider. Dark foliage and double purple blooms.

Nisqually Warrior. Tailored Supreme foliage, dark blue semi-double flowers.

Nymph Fly. Dark, satiny, spooned leaves. Fluted, dark blue single flowers.

October. Single purple blooms. Soft, pliable, longifolia foliage with orange variegations.

Oh My. Dark blue flowers; some stems have both double and single blooms. Plain, pointed foliage.

Oneida. Variegated leaves and double dark blue flowers.

Ozark Blue. Notched foliage. Royal blue double blooms.

Pacific Mermaid. Dark quilted leaves. Flowers are dark blue and double.

Patriot. Tailored leaves. Ruffled, deep blue, semi-double flowers.

Plum Purple. Round, true purple double blooms and tailored foliage.

Purpleable. Dark leaves have red backs. Flowers are purple and double.

Purple Boys. Double deep purple blooms. Very dark, red-backed foliage.

Purple Flattery. Shiny strawberry foliage. Double black-purple blooms.

Purple Pansy. Plain green foliage. Dark purple Geneva blooms.

Purple Reflection. Quilted strawberry leaves. Purple Geneva flowers.

Purple Smoke. Quilted and variegated leaves. Flowers are smoky purple doubles.

Rhapsodie Elfriede. Dark blue single blooms and quilted foliage.

Rhapsodie Maria. Girl leaves. Single, dark violet flowers.

Rhapsodie Sophia. Violet blue single blooms, round foliage.

Royal Fluff. Holly-like leaves. Fluffy, deep purple double blooms.

Royal Legend. Dark, ruffled leaves and dark purple double Geneva flowers.

Royal Mountbatten. Dark, quilted leaves. Blooms are fluted purple doubles.

Royal Token. Dark, ruffled leaves. Double purple fringed flowers.

Savoy Blue. Tailored leaves and dark blue Geneva blooms.

Say When. Dark, holly-like leaves. Frilled, pansy purple double flowers.

Sultry Purple. Glossy leaves. Dark maroon-purple flowers have curly edges.

The General. Tailored foliage. Flowers are semi-double purple stars.

Velvet Shadows. Wavy leaves. Ruffled purple single Geneva flowers.

Westdale Purple Mountain. Double purple flowers and long pointed strawberry foliage.

Westwind's Jill. Dark, ruffled leaves. Blooms are frilled deep purple and double.

RED

Ainsi Beau. Semi-double clear mauve. Strawberry, red-backed foliage.

Aurora's Fairest. Ruffled red double flowers. Wavy, cupped, glossy foliage.

Betsy Ross. Large double flowers of fuchsia red. Quilted, heart-shaped foliage.

Bullseye. Tailored leaves. Single star Geneva flowers are fuchsia-red.

Canadian Centennial. Plain green foliage. Double red Geneva blooms.

Cherry City. Single fuchsia star flowers. Tailored foliage.

Cherry Cordial. Semi-double red star blooms and tailored foliage.

Christmas Holly. Fancy dark leaves. Double burgundy red blooms.

Claret. Dark leaves and double burgundy red flowers.

Dixie Magic. Dark, ruffled, variegated leaves. Blooms are frilled red and double.

Dotty Red. Frilled double red flowers and dark, wavy leaves.

Echo Red. Flowers are fuchsia-red and semi-double. Dark green, quilted foliage.

Elegant. Semi-double, ruffled red flowers. Dark, red-backed leaves.

Essex. Variegated leaves and double red blooms.

Fiery Jewel. Tailored leaves. Fiery red, semi-double star flowers.

Fire Hazard. Full double, bright fuchsia-red blooms. Deep green, quilted foliage.

Flick Too. Double cerise to rose red blossoms. Ruffled, pointed foliage.

Fox Fire. Double red blooms and medium green, girl foliage.

Fuchsia Sparks. Large fuchsia star blooms and tailored foliage. Large grower.

Fuchsine Pink. Flowers are a deep red-pink. Blue-green, wavy leaves.

Garnet. Double, deep garnet red flowers. Shiny strawberry foliage.

Gertrude Honey. Wavy, bright red double blooms and shiny, dark foliage.

Glitter Top. Deep rose-red frilled double blossoms. Dark, ruffled foliage.

Gorgeous. Deep but bright fuchsia double flowers. Semi-wavy, deep green strawberry foliage.

Grape Violet. Heavily quilted strawberry leaves. Dark red-purple double flowers.

Heartaches. Single fuchsia red blooms are frilled. Wavy green foliage.

Hi Fi. Intense fuchsia-red star blooms. Tailored foliage.

"Hi Gail". Flowers are double rosy red. Dark green, pointed, red-backed foliage.

Hi Good Lookin. Wavy dark leaves. Frilled, velvety maroon double blooms.

High Voltage. Double burgundy red flowers and forest green, moderately waved foliage.

Hot One. Fuchsia star blooms. Heart-shaped, dark green foliage.

Janie. Pointed, quilted, scalloped leaves. Dark red double flowers.

Lili Posa. Tailored leaves. Blooms are double and a deep red-orchid color.

Lisa D. Dark, slightly quilted leaves. Red-purple double blooms.

Little Rogue. Quilted, slightly spooned leaves. Wavy, double flowers are fuchsia-red.

Lit Up. Wavy leaves. Fuchsia-red, semi-double blooms.

Lora. Quilted leaves. Bright red-orchid double flowers.

Madam Woo. Double fuchsia star flowers. Round, dark green, red-backed, strawberry foliage.

Ming. Wavy red, semi-double blooms. Rippled foliage.

Minnie. Girl leaves and double fuchsia blooms.

Molten Fire. Intense red double flowers. Quilted, dark green leaves have red backs.

Moonlight Madness. Flowers are double and fuchsia-red. Dark Green, red-backed, quilted foliage.

Mr. R. Double reddish purple blooms. Symmetrical, tailored foliage.

New Yorker. Tailored leaves have red backs. Flowers are double red.

Painted Jewel. Vivid red double blooms. Dark wavy leaves have red backs.

Paul Bunyan. Plain green foliage. Raspberry red, double star flowers.

Persian Glory. Large, semi-double, frilled red blooms. Broad, ruffled and variegated foliage.

Philly Dilly. Full double light plum-colored flowers. Dark green, slightly quilted foliage. Large grower.

Plum Cluster. Red-violet double star flowers. Dark, quilted foliage.

Prairie Rose. Large semi-double rose red flowers. Tailored, medium green foliage.

Prince Royal. Red-lavender, semi-double star Geneva flowers.

Rage. Tailored leaves and double magenta blooms.

Range Rider. Fuchsia red blooms and dark, glistening foliage.

Red Choice. Sport of Purple Choice. Double red blooms with dark, tailored foliage.

Red Frost. Dark red, frilled blooms. Shiny, wavy foliage.

Red Gem. Red-backed leaves. Flowers are fuchsia red Geneva star singles.

Reverie In Wine. Single red-purple blooms. Flat, wavy-edged foliage.

Rhapsodie Ramona. Single Bordeaux red flowers. Rounded, tailored leaves.

Ring-A-Ling. Supreme foliage. Double red flowers.

Roehr's Delight Magenta. Tailored foliage and magenta blooms.

Rosamont. Dark, tailored leaves. Rosy fuchsia, double flowers.

Rose Sprig. Full double, rosy fuchsia blooms. Tailored foliage.

Rose Wine. Double rosy wine blooms. Medium to dark green, shiny foliage.

Rosy Hue. Quilted leaves. Deep magenta, semi-double star flowers.

Royal Flush. Semi-double red-purple blooms and quilted, pointed leaves. Plant is compact but grows large.

Royal Jester. Dark, wavy leaves. Frilled burgundy single.

Royal Plum. Notched dark leaves and double mauve blooms.

Ruby. Dark tailored leaves. Fuchsia single flowers.

Rustic Red. Plain green foliage. Fuchsia flowers are double.

Scroll. Fringed red-purple single blossoms.

Shirred Mod. Heavily frilled double fuchsia flowers and dark strawberry foliage.

Sky Blue Pink. Quilted leaves. Flowers are light red-orchid doubles.

Spirit of 76. Quilted leaves. Red-purple semi-double blooms.

Standing Ovation. Variegated leaves and double crimson flowers.

Star Attraction. Dark, ruffled leaves. Frilled, fuchsia star flowers.

Star Daisy. Tiny leaves and single red-pink star flowers.

Striking. Shiny, dark leaves. Rosy fuchsia double Geneva blooms.

Sunrise Chalet. Variegated leaves. Double claret-red blooms.

Sunset Sky. Double, deep raspberry bloom and almost black foliage on a compact plant.

Susan Leslie. Quilted leaves. Rosy fuchsia double flowers.

Timmy. Dark, shiny leaves. Fuchsia star blooms.

Twilight Galaxy. Wavy, dark green leaves. Double fuchsia star flowers.

U-All-Come. Quilted leaves. Blooms are dark maroon doubles.

Valencia. Dark leaves and double raspberry-red flowers.

Vermilion Lake. Bright fuchsia star flowers. Dark green, veined, tailored foliage.

Victorian. Slightly wavy leaves. Single, fringed maroon Geneva flowers.

Westdale Lavender Sparkle. Plain green foliage. Red-lavender single Geneva blooms.

Wham Bang. Dark, glossy leaves and double cerise blooms.

Wine Bouquet. Double wine-red flowers and tailored, quilted foliage.

Winter Wine. Ruffled leaves. Single, wine red star Geneva flowers.

Your Pal. Dark, quilted, pointed leaves. Flowers are red-orchid Genevas.

Zulu Dancer. Shiny, wavy leaves. Tulip-shaped frilled single flowers are wine-black.

PINK

Ann Rutledge. Broad, flat leaves. Deep pink double blooms.

Ann Slocum. Very dark, rippled leaves. Rich pink wavy double flowers.

Arbutus Pink. Frosted pink single blooms. Quilted, flat, dark green foliage.

Autumn Russet. Dark, wavy leaves and russet pink double flowers.

Baby Pink. Bright pink full double. Small, glossy, dark green foliage.

Beau Bait. Full double ruffled pink flowers. Fern green, wax-like foliage.

Beau Catcher. Dark leaves and deep pink double blooms.

Beauty Spot. Dark, quilted leaves. Flowers are coral pink doubles.

Best Yet. Dark, wavy leaves and dark pink double blooms.

Blissful. Plain foliage. Double dark pink flowers.

Blush Love. Dark tailored leaves and blush pink double blossoms.

Bonnie B. Heart-shaped leaves. Flowers are double pink.

Breathless Pink. Double pink flowers, plain leaves.

California. Dark, ruffled leaves. Fringed pink double blooms.

Cherry Jubilee. Deeply serrated, heart-shaped foliage. Full double flowers of creamy pink.

Cloud Cap. Double pink blooms and plain green, tailored leaves.

Colorado Carnation. Double flowers are light pink. Scalloped, wavy foliage on a large plant.

Comarc. Dark, quilted leaves with red backs. Rose pink double blooms.

Constance Beth. Double rose pink flowers and ruffled, pointed foliage. Grows large.

Coral Glow. Full double blooms are a deep coral pink. Dark foliage and a small plant.

Cradle Song. Tiny, fuzzy leaves and double light pink blossoms.

Czarina. Large, double, fiery deep pink. Dark, tailored foliage.

Dandy Pink. Light green foliage. Pink double star flowers.

Deanna. Flowers are medium pink doubles. Medium green, plain foliage.

Ding-A-Ling. Notched, pointed leaves and bright pink double flowers.

Dramatic. Deep rose double blooms. Medium green, quilted foliage.

Early Show. Double clear pink blossoms and plain, quilted foliage.

Easter Hymn. Ruffled leaves. Magnolia-textured double pink flowers.

Easy Living. Round leaves. Wavy cerise single blooms.

Edith. Slightly wavy, notched leaves. Double pink flowers are frilled and fluted.

Egyptian Rose Garden. Dark leaves and dark rose-pink double blooms.

Eileen Johnson. Dark, ruffled leaves. Fringed double flowers are intense pink.

Elusive. Dark green, red-backed, tailored leaves. Double medium pink flowers.

Eveleth. Girl leaves. Frilled pink double blossoms.

Eyeful. Tailored leaves and double rose pink flowers.

Fanfare. Broad, bronzy leaves. Tufted raspberry pink star flowers.

Florista. Full double medium pink blooms. Notched foliage.

Frilly Billy. Frilled and ruffled pink blooms. Tailored foliage.

Gallant. Large rose pink double flowers. Dark green, quilted leaves.

Giant Step. Semi-double vivid pink flowers. Glossy, heart-shaped leaves. Plant grows 16 inches and more across.

Gleam. Dark longifolia leaves. Flowers are double rose pink.

Gorgeous Jewel. Dark, tailored, red-backed leaves. Deep pink double flowers.

Helen Daly. Frosty medium pink double flowers. Pointed, tailored foliage on a compact plant.

Help. Plain green foliage and large double pink blooms.

Hot Drops. Hot pink double flowers. Tailored, pink and green variegated foliage.

I Spy. Glossy, round, compact foliage. Flowers are deep pink doubles.

Jingle Bells. Slightly rippled leaves. Frilled raspberry-rose double blooms.

Joy Pink. Strawberry leaves and double rose pink blossoms.

Joy Ringer. Dark, quilted leaves. Flowers are double cerise pink.

Kentucky Breeze. Tailored leaves. Double cerise rose flowers.

Kim. Wavy leaves and ruffled double pink blooms.

Kramer's Sculptured Charm. Flowers are double cerise pink. Quilted, waxy foliage.

Lady Luck. Black-green, girl leaves. Frilled pink double blossoms.

Lady Ship. Large semi-double pink flowers. Plain green foliage.

Las Vegas. Double blooms are an intense pink. Black-green, glossy, quilted foliage.

Le Grand Fluff. Double pink star flowers. Light green, shiny foliage.

Legacy. Plain green foliage. Flowers are double pink Genevas.

Lilian Jarrett. Flowers are peach pink doubles. Variegated, heart-shaped leaves.

Los Angeles. Ruffled leaves and double pink blooms.

Louis Noble. Variegated leaves. Flowers are dark pink doubles.

Love-N-Beauty. Quilted, tailored foliage. Deep raspberry pink blooms.

Madelaine. Rosy pink double flowers. Slightly fluted foliage.

Many Frills. Frilled double flowers are strawberry pink. Dark, slightly wavy foliage.

Marble Pink. Double medium pink blooms. Variegated foliage never turns plain green.

Marble Rose. Double rose pink blooms. Permanently variegated leaves.

Mary B. Wavy, quilted leaves with red backs. Double curly pink blooms.

Maryum's Rose. Double flowers are rose pink and fringed. Ruffled foliage.

Miss America. Full double pink blooms. Dark green leaves.

Miss Arkansas. Wavy foliage. Double ruffled dark rose pink.

Missouri Lewis and Clark. Wavy pink star flowers. Girl foliage.

Missouri Melody. Tailored foliage. Light pink Geneva star blooms.

Misty. Soft rose full double flowers. Light green, pointed foliage.

Moon Crest. Bright pink semi-double blooms and dark green leaves.

Moon Poppy. Double flowers are light pink. Slightly quilted foliage.

Mozart. Serrated leaves. Fringed peach pink double blossoms.

Nancy Darling. Clear pink single flowers. Plain dark green foliage with red backs.

Ozark Rose. Rose pink double blooms. Very dark, plain foliage.

Paris Pink. Wavy leaves and deep pink fringed double flowers.

Patti. Quilted leaves. Fringed blossoms are medium pink doubles.

Peach Imp. Round leaves and peach colored blooms.

Peach Ruffy. Pointed foliage. Semi-double ruffled peach blooms.

Peach Satin. Double flowers are peach pink. Tailored foliage.

Peachy Keen. Double fringed peach pink blossoms and notched, girl foliage.

Persian Rose. Quilted leaves. Slightly frilled deep pink double flowers.

Persian Sensation. Variegated leaves. Double frilled blooms of rose pink.

Persian Sunrise. Tricolor leaves—green, cream, and pink. Salmon pink double blooms.

Persian Surprise. Variegated leaves and pink double flowers.

Philly. Tailored leaves. Flowers are semi-double and rose pink.

Pink Cameo. Blooms are double pink. Round, dark, small foliage.

Pink Carnation. Dark, quilted leaves. Slightly fringed pink double blossoms.

Pink Carnival. Tailored leaves. Semi-double pink star flowers.

Pink Dale. Strawberry leaves and double frilled pink blossoms.

Pink Dappled. Girl foliage. Deep pink double blooms.

Pink Heritage. Tailored leaves. Flowers are rose pink double star Genevas.

Pink N'Pretty. Light pink single blooms and quilted foliage.

Pink Pansy. Tailored leaves and hot pink double blooms.

Pink Panther. Dark, tailored leaves. Double flowers are shocking pink.

Pink Pirate. Double deep pink flowers and very dark, glossy foliage.

Pink Polly. Double medium rose pink blooms. Quilted, serrated, pointed foliage.

Pink Princess. Bright but soft pink double and semi-double flowers. Deep green, semi-glossy foliage.

Pink Reflection. Delicate pink semi-double blossoms. Glossy, medium green foliage.

Pink Ripple. Large pink flowers are semi-double. Plain green, tailored foliage.

Pink Sir. Dark, ruffled leaves and double fringed pink blooms.

Pink Spread. Slightly notched foliage. Fluffy pink double blooms.

Pink Velvet. Pink double flowers. Dark, tailored foliage.

Pippin Pink. Pink double flowers and Supreme foliage.

Playmate. Frilled semi-double pink star flowers. Glossy foliage.

Powder Pink. Full double dusty pink flowers and ruffled foliage.

Princess Pat. Dark strawberry leaves. Double pink Geneva blooms.

Pucker Up. Dark, quilted leaves. Double pink star flowers.

Regina. Dark, quilted leaves. Pink double blooms.

Remembrance. Quilted leaves and double pink flowers.

Rhapsodie Annette. Flowers are pink and semi-double. Rounded, girl foliage.

Rhapsodie Claudia. Large clear pink single flowers. Flat, plain green leaves.

Rhapsodie Gisela. Small, dark green leaves and single pink blooms.

Risque. Dark, wavy leaves. Frilled pink double blooms.

Romp. Nearly black, holly-like leaves. Fringed pink double flowers.

Rose Marie. Strawberry foliage. Frilled double blooms are deep rose pink. Small plant.

Ruckus. Large semi-double star flowers of medium pink. Medium green, slightly notched foliage.

Ruth B. Dark, quilted foliage and double medium pink blooms.

Sheba. Large rose pink double flowers. Dark green, tailored leaves.

Shebang Supreme. Heavy, notched leaves. Double pink, daisy-like flowers.

Shell Pink. Quilted leaves and fringed light pink double blooms.

Show Down. Double wavy-petalled pink flowers. Foliage is slightly notched, medium green, and quilted.

Siam Rose. Double rosy pink blooms. Medium green, slightly quilted foliage. Small to medium sized plant.

Silver Cameo. Variegated leaves and double shell pink flowers.

Sis Gee. Double pink blooms and girl foliage.

Sky-High Pink. Double, ruffled, light pink blossoms. Serrated, quilted, bright green leaves have red backs.

Smashing. Large, fully double, deep pink flowers. Lightly quilted, bronzy foliage.

Softique. Plain green foliage. Fluffy, baby pink, double blossoms.

Sophisticated. Light pink semi-double to double blooms. Light green, ruffled leaves on a large plant.

Splashy Rose. Medium pink flowers are double. Dark, tailored, quilted foliage.

Spring Bouquet. Quilted leaves. Semi-double, rose-pink flowers.

Springtime Sweetheart. Double, round light pink blossoms. Quilted foliage.

Stage. Double pink bloom. Plain foliage.

Stand Out. Tailored leaves. Double pink Geneva flowers.

Star Fire. Dark, wavy leaves. Fringed, shocking pink semi-double blooms.

Strawberry Rose. Shiny, dark leaves. Rose-pink double flowers.

Sugar Ice. Heavily quilted leaves. Single pink Geneva star blooms.

Sunday. Double pink bloom. Medium green, tailored foliage.

Supremacy. Dark leaves and double blooms of deep pink.

Sweet Charlotte. Semi-double baby pink bloom. Plain foliage.

Sweetheart Roses. Tailored, heart-shaped, variegated foliage. Deep pink double flowers.

Tassel. Full double deep pink blooms. Red-backed, glossy, plain foliage.

Terrific. Quilted leaves. Flowers are fluted pink doubles.

Thelma Usinger. Quilted leaves and medium pink double blooms.

The Mountaineer. Dark foliage. Double delicate pink flowers.

Tioga. Large double pink blooms. Light green, tailored leaves. Medium to large grower.

Trilby. Double pink blooms. Small plant.

Triple Threat. Round strawberry leaves and double pink flowers.

True Delight. Dark, slightly wavy leaves. Red-pink double.

Variegated Pin Up. Ruffled, variegated foliage. Double ruffled pink blooms.

Variegated Pink Spoon. Variegated leaves and double pink flowers.

Violet Harmony. Pink-lavender curly single blossoms.

Wanted. Dark, ruffled leaves. Fringed deep pink double flowers.

Wind Chimes. Soft pink single star flowers. Compact, tailored foliage.

Wincor. Dark leaves. Round pink double blooms.

Xtra New. Dark, quilted leaves. Medium pink, semi-double star flowers.

Yes Ma'am. Scalloped girl foliage. Deep pink double, water lily-type bloom.

ORCHID AND LAVENDER

Big Polly. Plain green foliage. Very large single orchid blooms.

Bishop's Violet. Spooned leaves. Double violet star flowers.

Calapooya. Tailored Supreme foliage. Large double orchid blooms.

Carefree. Plain green foliage and lavender double flowers.

Coralie. Large double lilac blooms. Tailored foliage.

Dreamster. Dark leaves. Light violet-blue double flowers.

Evagene. Plain green foliage. Flowers are double lavender-pink.

Floral Fantasy. Red-backed leaves. Large double lilac blooms.

Harvest Time. Dark Leaves. Semi-double, dark lavender Geneva blooms.

Hyman. Double vibrant lilac blooms and plain, tailored foliage.

Jewel Box. Rose-lavender blooms. Tailored foliage.

Jim Dandy. Flowers are double, medium rose-purple. Quilted, light green foliage.

Ki Ki. Fluted leaves and frilled, rose-lavender, double flowers.

Lavender Blossom Time. Ruffled double lilac blooms. Medium green, slightly wavy foliage.

Lavender Fluff. Double lavender blooms have ruffled edges. Tailored, medium green foliage with red backs.

Lilac Bouquet. Large clusters of double lilac flowers. Tailored foliage. Grows large.

Lucky Plum. Double plum-lavender flowers. Plain foliage.

Lulu Bell. Large, full, double deep lavender blooms. Very small plant.

Rancho D. Plain green foliage and double orchid flowers.

Serieta. Variegated leaves. Lavender pink double blooms with curly petals.

Star of Eve. Quilted leaves that sometimes spoon. Flowers are violet star Genevas.

Susy's Lady Mink. Girl foliage. Single lavender-violet fantasy blooms.

Veronica. Double violet star flowers. Medium green, semi-wavy foliage.

Wendy Sue. Quilted leaves. Double violet star Geneva blooms.

Westwind's Nasheba Springtime. Heart-shaped, serrated leaves. Orchid single star flowers.

Wisteria. Double lavender blooms. Plain, glossy foliage.

BICOLOR AND MULTICOLOR

Acadian. Light lilac semi-double flowers have white edges. Tailored foliage.

African Princess. Semi-double blooms of dark purple with frilled green edges. Ruffled foliage.

After Sunset. Semi-double blue star flowers with rose and cerise markings. Wavy leaves.

Alakazam. Semi-double flowers are a combination of flashy reds and purples. Quilted foliage.

Alice Blue. Variegated leaves, light blue and white double flowers.

Allie. Flowers are medium pink double with white petal edges. Quilted, tailored foliage.

Althea C. Spooned, heart-shaped leaves and deep red-purple, two-toned, double flowers.

Amigo. Lavender flowers have purple-tipped petals. Tailored foliage.

Amulet. Dark foliage. White double blooms with blue markings.

Ann B. Scalloped foliage. Single white flowers have deep lavender eyes and edges.

April Lilac. Tailored leaves. Double blooms are a lilac bi-color.

April Showers. Blue and white semi-double star flowers.

Athena. Fringed, fully double, rose form blooms are white with narrow blue petal edges. Dark, glossy, quilted leaves.

Aurora's Innocent. Semi-double white bloom with pink eye. Quilted foliage on a large plant.

Aurora's Pink Lady. Double, light to medium pink. Plain foliage. A strong grower.

Aurora's Queen Anne. Double white flowers have a trace of pink. Quilted reddish foliage. Plant grows large.

Baby Doe. Double medium pink with chartreuse edge on buds. Scalloped foliage. Makes a large plant.

Banner Year. Powder blue single flowers with deeper blue centers. Dark foliage.

Bellaire. White semi-double blooms with blue petal markings. Plain foliage.

Belle of Louisville. Dark quilted leaves. White double flowers are tinted lavender.

Betty Little. Quilted leaves. Double lavender flowers have darker petal tips.

Big D. Semi-double to double wine purple flowers. Flat, quilted, tailored foliage. Small to medium sized plant.

Biscayne. Light blue single flowers have darker veins and slight white edge. Dark, round, quilted foliage.

Bit O'Heaven. Blue-lavender single flowers have rays of deeper color.

Black Congo. Bronzy, quilted leaves. Single flowers are very dark wine-red with gold edges.

Blizzard. White double blooms are marked with pink. Tailored foliage. Small to medium sized plant.

Blue Butterfly. Large, double, pale blue blooms have notched green petal edges. Medium-sized, quilted foliage. Small grower.

Blue Cup. Dark, tailored foliage. Shaded light blue double blooms.

Blue-Eyed Daisy. Semi-double white bloom with blue center. Tailored foliage.

Blue Frost. Double bright blue blossoms have white edges. Glossy foliage.

Blue Ice. Tailored foliage. Double blue and white flowers.

Blue Owl. Single powder blue blooms with darker top petals. Medium green, pointed leaves.

Blue Power. Flowers are single, medium blue with lighter shadings. Plain, pointed foliage. Grows large.

Blue Puff. Tailored leaves. Blue and white double flowers.

Blue Reverie. Semi-double light blue with lighter blue fringe on petal edges. Quilted, wavy leaves.

Blue Rim. Wavy, quilted leaves. Ruffled double white flowers with blue edges.

Blue Vanessa. Double white blooms infused with blue. Quilted, semi-Supreme foliage.

Blue Willow. Emerald green, quilted leaves. Blue and white, six-petaled star flowers.

Brigadoon. Semi-double, bright rose-red with white petal edges. Plain, quilted, pointed foliage.

Brightness. Large, dark cerise-pink double flowers. Dark green, tailored foliage.

Broken Arrow. Double orchid flowers have purple petal edges. Large, girl-type foliage.

Buccaneer. Dark maroon-red, two-toned double blooms. Plain leaves.

Bumble Bee. Dark leaves. Pink semi-double flowers with a trace of gold edging.

Burgundy Wasp. Dark, red-backed leaves. Single burgundy red flowers with darker petal tips.

Cabaret. Double dark red, white fringed blooms. Wavy foliage.

Calico Wasp. Quilted leaves. Lavender and purple fantasy-type bloom.

California Skies. Double dark rose with white edge. Quilted, fringed foliage.

Cameo Rose. Rosy pink double flowers with deep rose centers. Tailored foliage.

Cameroon. Ruffled leaves. Flowers are cerise and red two-tone singles with gold edges.

Candy Divinity. Tailored foliage. Blooms are white shaded light pink with darker pink markings.

Candy Kid. Dark, holly-like leaves with red backs. Deep pink double flowers have green edges.

Candy Lips. Large full double white blooms are pencil edged in red.

Cape Cod. Double white with blue eye and green edge. Holly-like leaf.

Carillon. Tailored leaves. Double, fluted lavender bi-color Geneva blooms.

Carnival Boy. Plain green foliage. White and light blue single star flowers.

Caroline. Tailored leaves. White double blooms with pink shading.

Cartwheel. Quilted, variegated leaves. Pink star single flower with dark eye.

Cascade Orchid. Soft pink with rose center. Ruffled, dark foliage.

Chapel Pink. Flowers are double pink with white edges. Glossy, scalloped foliage.

Charade. Double fuchsia pink blooms with blue markings. Slightly wavy, red-backed foliage.

Charmglow. Tailored leaves. Fluted, shaded, rose and lavender double flowers have maroon markings.

Cherry Flip. Ruffled leaves. White double blooms with fringed fuchsia edges.

Chity-Chity Bang-Bang. Double white with purple on petal edges and sides. Quilted foliage. Grows large.

Chivalry. Blue bloom with white edge. Plain foliage.

Chocolate Chip. Plain green foliage. Double lavender-pink flowers with fantasy markings.

Cimarron. Dark, holly-like leaves. Lavender double with green petal edges.

Circus Girl. Blue-and-white-striped blooms. Girl foliage.

Clydene. Plain green foliage. Semi-double orchid bi-color blooms.

Cockatoo. Tailored leaves. White double flowers have rose centers.

Color Carnival. Small dark leaves. Semi-double pink with red markings.

Colorado Rosebud. Double, dark, two-toned pink with darker center. Serrated foliage.

Colorscope. Round, flat leaves. White and purple double flowers have green edges.

Columbia View. Silvery pink flowers have blue, orchid, and rose red markings. Tailored foliage.

Coralene. Tailored leaves. Deep pink double with deeper pink border.

Coral Reef Sport. White and coral pink double. Tailored foliage.

Corona. Quilted, wavy, strawberry leaves. Ruffled and fluted white double with red edge.

Costa Brava. Variegated leaves. Semi-double red flowers with darker petal tips.

Cotillion Variegated. Red and white fringed double. Shiny, wavy foliage.

Count Down. Large blue double flowers edged in white. Strong grower.

Cream Pink. Almost black leaves. Light pink double with coral pink petal tips.

Crepe Sunburst. Six-petalled shaded light plum with cerise edges. Tailored foliage.

Crepe Sunrise. Tailored foliage. Six-petalled flowers combine shades of pink and rose.

Crepe Sunset. Tailored leaves. Shaded cerise-plum with six petals.

Crown of Gold. Double light lavender with darker bands. Plain foliage.

Crown Prince. Single dark purple with mauve pink curved markings like a pansy. Cupped up and pointed foliage. Grows large.

Cynthia. Quilted leaves. Fringed pink, semi-double bi-color blooms.

Dairy Maid. Semi-double white with lavender center. Tailored light green leaves.

Dancer. Double lavender blooms with dark edges. Large flowers.

Daphne. Giant semi-double pink blooms are flecked with blue. Deep green foliage. Strong grower.

Dark-Eyed Babe. Dark leaves. Lavender single flowers have maroon edges.

Dating Game. Very dark quilted leaves. Pink and blue blooms have darker veins.

Dawn Purple. Double plum purple flowers have big yellow eyes. Red-backed foliage.

Deep Flame. Shiny, round, wavy leaves. Fringed, two-toned red double.

Del Crest. Tailored leaves. Purple double with red purple edges.

Delft Imperial. Delft blue double blooms have a white fringe on petal edges. Notched foliage.

Dimpled Darling. Single pink, purple-marked blooms. Plain foliage.

Ding-A-Ling. Modified girl foliage. Single lavender with purple markings.

Discovery. Single shaded lilac. Quilted, ruffled, dark foliage.

Don. Single, dark, velvety violet with darker petal edge. Quilted foliage.

Donnie Joe. Tailored leaves. Wavy white star flowers with lavender and blue markings.

Double Crest. Tailored leaves. Double purple star flowers have red-purple petal edges.

Double Samoa. Double purplish blue flowers with lighter spots. Tailored foliage.

Double Scroll. Tailored leaves. Purple semi-double with red-purple edges.

Double Seafoam. Medium blue double with white edge. Ornamental foliage.

Double Sir Lancelot. Two-toned double, lavender and purple.

Dr. Jekyll and Mr. Hyde. Long, wavy leaves. Purple and white variable double.

Dreamy Frills. Girl-type leaves. Frilled, crested white blooms with pink markings.

Duet. Large, white-edged, bright blue double blooms. Tailored foliage.

Early Spring. Dark, glossy leaves and shaded pink, semi-double flowers.

Edge of Night. Semi-double white with dark blue petal edges. Notched foliage.

Eleanor Ann. Single dark pink bloom with deeper eye. Scalloped and quilted foliage.

English Rose. Plain green foliage. Fringed, shaded, pink double.

Escapade. Large double blooms of deepest blue with rosy overtones. Dark foliage.

Family Affair. Quilted foliage. White-centered rose pink, semi-double star.

Fantasy Rose. Rose red double, shaded lighter rose. Dark, symmetrical foliage.

Firebird. Fringed single bloom—brilliant red center with white border. Wavy foliage. Small plant.

Fleecy Cloud. Clear pink semi-double with white petal edges. Quilted foliage.

Fling. Wavy dark leaves. Orchid double flowers with pink markings.

Fly Away. Semi-double red with white petal edges. Medium green, tailored foliage.

Fluff Stuff. Dark, wavy leaves. Ruffled pink and fuchsia double.

Flying Saucer Red. Quilted leaves. Fringed red single flowers have deeper edges.

Foggy Weather. Double blue with silver edges.

Frathel's Alluring. Variegated girl leaves. Orchid and violet double.

Friendly Rival. Semi-double deep pink bloom with deeper eye. Dark green foliage.

Frilled Dandy. Creamy white semi-double with chartreuse petal edges. Top petals are green. Quilted, pointed foliage.

Frilled Velvet. Dark ruffled leaves. Flowers are frilled deep blue double with lighter edges.

Frosted Lilac. Medium green, serrated foliage. Semi-double rose-purple star flowers, marked with deep amethyst violet and cream.

Frosted Rose. Dark foliage. Double rose pink with darker top petals and Geneva edge.

Frosting. Tailored foliage. Frosty rose with wide band of white on the petals.

Fun City. Ruffled leaves. Pink and white fringed double.

Gaiety. Wavy dark leaves. Shaded frilled pink double.

Garnet Star. Double purple with petal tips frilled and edged in white.

Gay White. Double white and pink. Plain foliage on a large plant.

Gee Gee. Double, wavy, red-orchid bloom with white edge. Wavy foliage.

Giant Butterfly. Tailored leaves. Pastel pink semi-double with a darker pink eye.

Giant Amethyst. Tailored leaves. Large lavender flowers have darker edges.

Giddy-Up-Go. Double frilled pink with darker petal edges. Dark foliage.

Gilt Edge. Ruffled leaves. Bright blue double with green petal edges.

Glamour Doll. Dark, red-backed foliage. Full double light blush pink with rose pink petal edges.

Glittering Jewel. Deep pink double, fringed in green. Holly-like leaf. Grows large.

Globus Pallidus. Double light bluish lavender with darker petal edges. Plain foliage.

Going Places. Compact plant has dark, quilted, red-backed leaves. Grayish blue semi-double flowers have deeper centers.

Gold Coast. Holly-like leaves. Green-edged, double pink flowers.

Good Sport. Dark, hairy leaves. Double pink flowers have green edges.

Granger Garden's Pied Piper. Double blue-white. Plain foliage.

Greenbrier. Fringed white-and-blue-mottled double. Ruffled foliage.

Green Frills. Double fringed green flowers are tinged pale lavender. Quilted foliage.

Green Lace. Dark fluted leaves. Pink double blooms have gold edges.

Green Paint. Pink double flower with green fringed edge.

Green Rosette. Double green and white flowers. Tailored foliage. Makes a small plant.

Greetings. Slightly wavy leaves. Two-toned fuchsia semi-double flowers.

Gus. Double dark magenta flowers with purple streaks. Plain foliage.

Gypsy Star. Mottled lavender and white single flowers.

Hand Picked. Girl leaves. Pink double flowers with red markings.

Hapatica. White single flowers are rayed with lavender and purple. Dark green wavy leaves.

Happy Daze. Double pale pink flowers have reddish plum petal edges and tips. Plain foliage.

Harvest Time. Giant semi-double flowers are lavender edged in white.

Heavenly Stars. Peach pink semi-double flowers with dark rose edges.

Helen Van Zele. Ivory white semi-double blooms have a frosted pink tinge. Quilted, heart-shaped foliage.

Hidden Treasure. Wavy leaves. Frilled semi-double blue and white blooms.

Holiday Candle. Double, frilly cerise-red flowers with gold edges. Dark, red-backed foliage.

Holly Golightly. Semi-double lilac blooms have frilled green edges. Dark, glossy, holly-like foliage.

Honey Jewel. Double light pink with copper tones. Dark tailored foliage.

Icebreaker. Multi-colored leaves. Fringed, double, white flowers have purple edges.

Illini Cadet. Red, semi-double star flowers with white and green borders. Dark tailored foliage.

I'm So Blue. White and shades of blue from deepest to sky, double to semi-double. Tailored foliage.

Inca Chief. Fuchsia red double with wide white edge. Tailored strawberry foliage.

Inky Pink. Semi-double pink flowers splashed with purple. Red-backed foliage.

In Style. Pink semi-double with white edges. Tailored foliage.

Intensified Pride. Dark quilted leaves. Cerise blossoms have lighter streaks.

Irish Crochet. Olive green foliage. Frilled pink double blooms with green edges.

Jay Bee Gee. Wine-amethyst flowers with deep black-wine edge; pom-pom double bloom. Quilted, scalloped foliage.

Jayne Anne. Double medium pink with rose red shadings. Quilted, ruffled, pointed strawberry foliage.

Jazz. Double shaded lavender to deep wine. Pointed, dark green foliage.

Jeepers Creepers. Standard foliage. Red, pink, and white double flowers.

Jennifer. Single cupped pale lavender with dark lavender and white to green edges. Longifolia foliage.

Jeweltone. Flat, semi-double rosy pink and raspberry flowers. Dark, flexible foliage.

Jimmy Watson. Single dark pink with purple flowers are sometimes streaked white. Heart-shaped leaves.

Joanne My Lady. Ruffled leaves. Pink double with green edges.

Joker. Dark, tailored leaves. Orchid double with blue markings.

Juan Tu. Quilted leaves. Pink single flowers have green petal edges.

Judy Ann. Small quilted, scalloped foliage. Double white bloom with shell pink center; some have green edges.

Julie B. Double shaded purple-blue. Tailored foliage.

Jungle Joy. Wavy leaves. Frilled red-and-white-striped single.

Kabuki Dream. Dark blue double with pink shadings. Dark leaves.

Kaneland Beauty. Ruffled leaves. Fluted blue and white single flowers.

Kansas City Chief. Quilted, ruffled leaves. Light red single star flowers have green edges.

Karachi. Dark quilted leaves. Plum bicolor double blooms with deeper petal edges and tips.

Kay Gaung. Two-toned pink double. Wavy foliage.

King's Jewels. Quilted wavy leaves. Fuchsia red double with deeper center.

Kismet. Small, tailored foliage. Full double white and pink bloom.

Kiwanda. Dark blue double flowers with green frilled edges. Shiny, almost black-red foliage.

Knit Wit. Fuchsia fantasy flower, ruffled and double with white edges. Dark, tailored foliage.

Kopikat. Compact plant with dark quilted leaves. Powder blue double flowers have darker centers.

Korean Princess. Two-toned reddish purple double flowers with white edges. Large, tailored foliage.

Kramer's Eclipse. Double dark blue with white-dotted edges. Glossy, quilted foliage. Grows large.

Kramer's Forever Yours. Double medium blue blooms have white edges. Quilted foliage. Grows large.

Kramer's Gem Dandy. Double medium and dark blue flowers. Quilted, waxy foliage.

Kramer's Liberty Bell. Medium blue double with white markings. Quilted, waxy foliage.

Kramer's Natural Blush. Double white flowers have pink shadings. Quilted foliage.

Kramer's Peek-A-Blue. Double fringed light blue with white edges. Quilted, pointed, glossy foliage. Grows large.

Kramer's Petti Point. Double fringed white flowers with pink centers and green edges. Quilted foliage.

Lady Beatrice. Double flowers are variable lilac and white. Tailored foliage.

Lady Bountiful. Single star flowers are pink with deep wine red borders. Girl foliage—dark, broad, and round.

Lady Helen. Crested, two-toned, fringed orchid blooms. Slightly fluted foliage.

Lakeland. Fluffy white semi-double flowers with blue markings. Tailored foliage.

Lavender Flair. Full double, deep lavender with dark orchid petal borders. Dark green, quilted, tailored foliage.

Lavender Fringe. Wavy leaves. White double flowers have lavender edges.

Lavender Gem. Very tailored plant. Double, brilliant red-orchid blooms with white edges. Plain foliage.

Le Chateau. Dark, quilted leaves. Shaded double pink star flowers.

Lee Belle. Crested petals in shades of orchid. Dark green, notched foliage.

Leola. Single, deep lavender-pink blooms with white edges. Quilted, pointed foliage.

Lightup. Bright double pink with darker edges. Dark green, tailored foliage.

Lilac Festival. Wavy leaves. Two-toned lilac semi-double blooms.

Lilac Glow. Quilted leaves. Double violet flowers have deeper petal tips.

Lilac Wonder. Double two-toned lavender, from pale to rosy. Ruffled girl foliage.

Lili Belle. Large semi-double fuchsia and white blossoms. Slightly wavy, scalloped foliage.

Linda Star. Variegated leaves. Fringed blue bi-color double flowers.

Lindora. Double pink with rosy top petals. Tailored foliage.

Lollipop. Semi-double, shaded pink with dark reddish pink center. Sometimes blooms will be solid red. Medium green shiny foliage.

Lone Star. Raspberry red single blooms with white markings. Color is variable.

Louise Black. Semi-double pale pink with coppery gold upper petal tips. Plain, tailored foliage. Grows large.

Lothario. Standard foliage. Flowers are hyacinth blue and lavender.

Lotsa Blue. Quilted, dark, red-backed leaves. Shaded powder blue semi-double blossoms.

Lovely One. Double ruffled light pink, shading to fuchsia in flower centers. Dark shiny foliage.

Lynne. Double shaded plum red star flowers. Tailored foliage.

Margie Jean. Pointed leaves. Bicolor red-violet single star flowers.

Martha B. Blooms are a combination of white, blue, lavender, and purple with white-green edges. Tailored foliage.

Mary Odell. Double deep pink flowers with lighter pink petal tips. Plain foliage.

Mattie Mae. Large magenta double with white petal edges. Medium green foliage. Large leaves.

Maud Maeo. Quilted, ruffled, variegated leaves. Light violet and orchid double blooms.

May Queen. Tufted single star flowers are shaded rose pink Genevas. Flexible foliage.

Maya. Wavy, olive green leaves. Soft lavender double flowers have darker markings.

Maytime. Double light pink star blooms with white petal backs. Medium green, quilted foliage.

Megan. Ruffled, variegated leaves. Pink bicolor double Geneva blooms.

Melanie. Bright fuchsia red double flowers are edged in white. Tailored foliage.

Mellow White. Tailored leaves. Double white flowers are tinged pink.

Melody. Large pink semi-double with white petal edges. Plain, tailored foliage.

Memory of Celilo. Tailored Supreme leaves. Very large, blue and white single blooms.

Merrie Lynn. Two-toned, ruffled, double pink blossoms. Serrated, red-backed, medium green, rounded leaves.

Michael A. Double white, purple, and lavender blooms. Scalloped foliage.

Midnight Echo. Tailored leaves. Double shaded purple Geneva flowers.

Midnight Snow. Wavy, quilted foliage. Variable blue and white blooms.

Milwaukee. Deep lavender semi-double with white petal edges. Dark green, tailored foliage.

Minerva. Tailored leaves. Double lavender bi-color blooms.

Mint Marble. Variegated leaves. Ruffled blue and white single flowers.

Missouri Country Capers. Pink to raspberry double with white petal edges. Dark shiny foliage.

Missouri Country Music. Dark, notched leaves. Frilled shaded cerise star flowers.

Missouri Genie. Plum blooms with white edge are single stars.

Missouri Hit or Miss. Quilted foliage. Double plum star flowers have purple and lavender shadings.

Missouri Peggie Sue. Modified girl foliage. Lavender, blue, and white blooms.

Missouri Pink Star. Plain green, tailored foliage. Single pink star flowers with white edges.

Missouri Twilight. Shaded cerise and lavender star blooms.

Molly 'O. Double white with sprinkling of rose in petals. Heart-shaped girl foliage.

Mom Dear. White star flowers are edged in dark blue.

Mom's Gingerbread. Frilly, semi-double fringed orchid-violet flowers are dotted with purple. Ruffled, marbled, shiny foliage.

Monique. Single lavender flowers with darker eyes. Plain, quilted foliage.

Moon Born. Double white star flowers are edged blue; centers are white. Symmetrical, quilted foliage.

Moon Magic. Single deep violet-purple with white petal edges. Plain, slightly pointed foliage.

Moon Walk. Double fuchsia with white border. Lightly quilted, pointed foliage.

Morning Light. Double lavender-speckled fantasy flowers. Plain, quilted foliage.

Mount Angel. Flowers are fully double and round, like fringed balls of white and green. Shiny green foliage, small plant.

Missouri Sing Along. Tailored foliage. Frilled, shaded, royal blue blooms.

Missouri Singing Rain. Girl foliage. Semi-double lavender flowers with darker markings.

Missouri Star Glow. Dark, quilted foliage. White star flowers with pink markings.

Missouri Surprise. Tailored foliage. Double frilled blue and purple star flowers.

Mrs. Pink. Plain green foliage. Two-toned pink blooms.

Mt. Smokie. Double medium blue flowers with white edges. Narrow, serrated, quilted foliage.

Muriel. Double large medium pink blooms sometimes are fluted with green. Shiny, medium green, plain foliage.

My Choice. Semi-double fuchsia star flowers have wide white petal edge. Tailored foliage.

My Lollipop. Cerise pink semi-double blooms with deeper centers. Shiny, wavy foliage.

Mysterious. Wavy light pink double with rose-purple petal tips.

Nancy Ann. Double white blooms with darker lavender centers and edges.

Neahkaie Treasure. Ruffled Supreme leaves. Flowers are frilled two-toned orchid.

Nettie Borrin. Blooms are shaped like sweet peas and are fringed singles with very pale blue fantasy markings and a heart-shaped pink inlay. Leaves are splashed with purple.

New Snow. Rippled leaves. Greenish white double flowers.

Nez Perce. Double white flowers are splotched with cerise and rose. Round, shiny, Supreme foliage with red backs.

Nimbus. Glossy fern green, compact foliage. Semi-double white and blue flowers.

Northern Breeze. Blue and white single blooms and large, ruffled foliage.

October Sunset. Single, bright hot pink to red blooms. Quilted, holly-type foliage.

O'Linda Sport. Girl leaves. Blue and white double flowers.

Orchid Corona. Two-toned orchid-purple single with fringed green petal edges. Tailored foliage.

Orchid Luster. Blooms are double lavender with darker borders. Quilted leaves.

Oriole Pink. Double pink with white petal edges. Light green, quilted foliage.

Our Nancy. White and azure blue double blooms. Plain, pointed leaves.

Outer Space. Tailored leaves. Lavender single star flowers with purple edges.

Ozark Queen. Dark foliage. Single pink to rose shaded star blooms.

Ozark Star. Quilted foliage. Semi-double pink to rose blooms.

Painted Wings. Pointed leaves. White single flowers have lavender markings.

Pam D. Shaded plum with white petal edges. Dark, red-backed foliage.

Pat Nixon. Dark foliage. Double plum star flowers with lighter edges.

Patricia Anne. Single, frilled, white star blooms with shaded purple edges. Soft, pliable, wavy apple green foliage.

Patrician. Blooms are fully double—dark purple with white edges. Quilted, pointed foliage.

Pat's Pet Supreme. Greenish white double blooms. Ruffled foliage.

Patty D. Tailored foliage. Semi-double frilled pink star flowers with white edges.

Peace Pink. Frilled apricot pink blooms are semi-double with deeper top petals. Heart-shaped foliage.

Peach Tips. Tailored leaves. Double magenta blossoms have peach edges.

Peacock Fancy. Tailored foliage. Shaded pink-lavender, cerise, purple, and blue blooms have green edges.

Peacock Strut. Quilted foliage. Flowers are double blue with wavy green edges.

Peace Valley. Bronze, wavy leaves. Bright pink single blooms with darker markings.

Pecks of Pink. Tailored leaves. Dark blue double blooms with pink dots.

Peggy. Single light pink star flowers with purple dots and splotches. Plain foliage.

Petit Fours. Slightly wavy leaves. Frilled white double flowers variably marked purple.

Petunia. Light pink blooms shade to dark centers. Light green, ruffled foliage.

Pied Piper. Blue and white full double flowers. Tailored foliage.

Pink Accent. Ruffled and variegated leaves. Pink and white double flowers.

Pink Diamond Correction. Vivid pink single with slight white petal edges. Smooth, moss green, heart-shaped foliage.

Pinkesque. Double pink with white petal edges. Flat, soft, scalloped foliage.

Pink Eye. Full double, ruffled white flowers with pale pink eyes. Heavy, scalloped foliage. Grows large.

Pink Love. Quilted leaves. Pink double blooms have pink and green edges.

Pinkie Pride. Shaded pink bloom is edged in red. Very dark, red-backed, heart-shaped foliage.

Pink N'Gold. Pink semi-double flowers have green and gold edges.

Pink Proliffity. Quilted leaves. Double light pink bicolor flowers.

Pink Rayed. Double pink blooms are dotted and striped purple. Large, glossy foliage.

Pink Shadows. Deep pink semi-double blooms shade to rose in centers. Quilted, slightly notched foliage.

Pink Vision. Double pink with thin white petal edge. Light green, slightly quilted foliage.

Pink Wedding. Delicate, full double blooms are pink with white edges. Medium green, tailored foliage.

Poodle Top. Fringed double lavender pink. Top petals are pale to rosy lavender with faint green tinge. Plain foliage.

Pop Art. Double bloom shades from reddish lavender to dark purple petal tips. Cupped foliage.

Preview. Broad leaves. Blooms are frilled pink double with darker eyes.

Prince of Peace. Fringed purple flowers with white edges and markings.

Proma. Double, fringed, pale orchid blooms have deeper eyes and white and green edges. Ruffled, heart-shaped foliage.

Purple Choice. Deep purple blooms with white petal edges.

Punch. Wavy leaves. Single orchid bicolor flowers.

Radiance. Semi-double blooms are iridescent red-purple with white edges. Quilted and pointed foliage.

Rainbow Jewel. Dark, tailored leaves. Rose double blooms with brighter edges.

Rainbow's End. Variegated leaves. Shaded salmon pink single flowers.

Red Choice. Bright single pink flowers have lighter frilled edges. Wavy, medium green foliage.

Red Rocket. Plain foliage. Semi-double red star flowers with pink markings.

Red Sparkle. Full double, fluted blossoms are bright red with white edges. Light green, wavy foliage.

Red Trinket. Red blooms have sparkling white edges. Dark, tailored foliage.

Rhapsodie Gigi. Semi-double white with blue band on petal edges. Plain, round foliage.

Rhapsodie Ophelia. Single, plum red blooms with darker centers. Plain, tailored foliage.

Rhapsodie Violetta. Two-toned rose-lavender single flowers. Tailored foliage.

Ridin' High. Semi-double white star flowers are lightly shaded with blue. Fern green foliage.

Ringlet. Semi-double pink blooms sometimes have darker petal edges. Plain foliage.

Roehr's Delight. Tailored foliage and shaded pink double flowers.

Rose Amethyst. Quilted Supreme foliage. Double amethyst purple blooms with violet petal tips.

Rose Crest. Wavy leaves. Flowers are ruffled white double with red edges.

Rose Fleur. Tailored, quilted, red-backed leaves. Rose flowers with deeper rose centers.

R. K. Paragon. Dark, quilted leaves. Double blooms are shaded raspberry pink.

Roseneath. Mauve pink double flowers are tinged with green. Dark, holly-like foliage.

Rose of Tralee. Coral rose double blooms have fringed green edges. Notched Supreme foliage.

Rose O'Regon. Semi-double coral-rose blooms are infused with white in the centers. Round, ruffled, shiny foliage.

Rose Reverie. Two-toned, fringed, bight rose-red semi-double flowers. Dark, tailored foliage.

Royalaire. Double royal blue with white edges. Plain, quilted foliage.

Royal Cluster. Plain, quilted foliage. Flowers do not fall when old. Single and semi-double light mauve blooms have deeper mauve edges.

Ruth Carey. Peach pink, semi-double, frilled blossoms. Tinges of white or green appear in some flowers. Shiny, forest green, quilted foliage.

Sabina. Dark, quilted leaves. Blooms are shaded lavender and purple singles.

Sally Ann. Dark, scalloped leaves. Light pink single flowers with darker centers.

Salmon Bicolor. Red-backed leaves. Salmon pink double blooms have darker petal tips.

Satellite Frills. Dark, slightly ruffled leaves. Semi-double, frilled, lavender star flowers with purple edges.

Satellite Pink. Semi-double pink blooms have a fuchsia band on the petal edges. Tailored foliage.

Satellite Shadows. Dark, tailored leaves. Fringed wine red single star flowers are rayed with lighter and deeper tones.

Satellite Star. Plain leaves. Fringed pink single star blooms have fuchsia edges.

Satin Doll. Plain green foliage. Very light pink blooms with chartreuse edges.

Satin Rouge. Ruffled, bronzy leaves. Rosy cerise single blooms; petals have red tips and gold edges.

Seafoam. Single, fringed, medium blue blooms have broad white edges—giving a pansy appearance. Quilted, wavy foliage on a small plant.

Sea Rose. Large wavy leaves. Single bicolor pink flowers with gold edges.

Secret Love. Dark leaves. Blooms are filled, semi-double, peach pink, with deeper edges.

Sheer Poetry. Moderately ruffled leaves. Baby pink double with rose petal edges.

Sherry Gail. Small, heart-shaped leaves. Two-toned double lavender blooms.

Shipshape. Bright rosy fuchsia double with white petal edges. Tailored foliage.

Shooting Star. Single bicolor pink star flowers have darker pink markings.

Silver Celebration. Two-toned lavender blooms with pink edges. Dark, quilted, heart-shaped foliage.

Silver Garland. Variegated leaves. Ruffled white blooms are double with purple edges.

Sip Stripe. Dark, hairy foliage. Shaded dark purple blooms.

Sissy Britches. Fringed, double, pale blue fantasy flowers are splashed with purple and have a pink overlay. Heart-shaped leaves. Grows large.

Sky Clipper. Semi-double blue flowers with white markings and touches of green.

Sky Jewel. Fluffy double white blooms with sky blue markings. Light green, tailored foliage.

Snow Flower. Double white and pink blooms. Plain foliage.

So Rare. Double flowers are pink with a white border. Dark green, quilted foliage.

Southern Cross. Quilted, ruffled leaves. Orchid pink bicolor flowers are double.

Sparkette. Double pink blooms often with blue dashes in petals. Dark, tailored foliage.

Sparky. Dark pointed leaves. Deep pink double flowers have raspberry red centers.

Spinner. Extra large reddish-lavender single flowers are edged with white. Deep green, tailored foliage.

Spring Lilac. Semi-double violet star flowers with deeper pencil edge on petals. Medium green, quilted foliage.

Star Boarder. Picotee leaves. Wavy light blue star blooms with darker blue edges.

Star Chimera. Compact, variegated leaves. Frilled single star flowers vary from pure white to white with wine red markings.

Star Cure. Slightly wavy foliage. Semi-double frilled light raspberry blooms with star markings.

Stardom. Dark leaves. Double pink star flowers have wine red markings.

Star Dream. Pink and red two-toned double star blooms. Medium green foliage on a large plant.

Star Flight. Tailored leaves. Semi-double rosy pink star blooms are marked white.

Starry Eyed. Waxy leaves. Red-centered white star flowers are semi-double.

Star Spray. Giant pink star flowers are edged in deeper pink. Strong grower.

Startling. Fantasy light lavender with blue flecks.

Stateliner. Double light pink star flowers have fuchsia pink edges.

Strawberry Ripple. Ruffled, tawny leaves. Shaded pink double flowers.

Sultry Rose. Very dark leaves. Double blooms are frilled rose pink to fuchsia.

Sun Up. Very dark quilted leaves. Shaded plum double blooms.

Susan. Tailored foliage. Pink semi-double flowers with cherry pink markings.

Susy's Lady Suzette. Girl foliage. Violet double blooms with darker petal tips.

Susy's Mr. Lucky. Dark foliage with pinched edges. Double violet flowers have darker edges and top petals.

Sweet Amethyst. Lavender-blue double blooms with thin white edges. Ruffled foliage.

Tejas. Bronzy green, tailored, slightly pointed foliage. Flowers are dark fuchsia with darker streaks, semi-double to double.

The Duchess. Dark, variegated, flat, girl foliage. Double blooms have mauve centers and wide purple-banded edges.

Theme Song. Wavy leaves. Medium pink double blooms with watermelon pink markings.

Tinted Clouds. Broad, wavy leaves. Fuchsia-edged frilled white double flowers.

Tipt. Single lavender with dark purple petal tips. Tailored foliage on a large plant.

Top Stars. Large pink star blooms with deeper centers. Shiny, medium green, quilted foliage. Grows large.

Touch of Spring. Ruffled, quilted leaves. Fringed white double blooms have green edges.

Trails West. Very dark leaves with red backs. Shaded pink semi-double flowers.

Traveler. Shades of rose to deep red semi-double blossoms. Ruffled foliage.

True Blue. Double, deep blue blooms are edged in crystal white. Slightly crimped, quilted foliage.

Trumpet Hybrid. Ruffled leaves. Blooms are double white with blue edges.

Tu Tu. Standard foliage. Light orchid and white single blooms.

U. C. Debbie. Tailored leaves. Double pink flowers with purple markings.

Uganda Trophy. Medium blue semi-double blooms are shaded and marked with white. Ruffled, bright green foliage.

Ultra Sport. Double pink flowers are streaked wtih fuchsia. Pointed foliage.

U. R. Kidden. Dark, quilted leaves. Wavy powder blue blooms with deeper centers.

Val's Bingo. Wavy leaves. Curly red double flowers sometimes have white markings.

Val's Sweet Dreams. Tailored, variegated leaves. Shaded pink double blooms.

Vanity Fair. Tailored, light green foliage. Full double flowers are lavender-pink with purple dots.

Venus. Plain green foliage. Red-lilac star blooms with deeper markings.

Victorian Jewel. Double lavender with purple border and gold petal edging. Dark, flexible foliage.

Victorian Lace. Dark leaves. Light orchid double with purple petal tips.

Violet Fair Sport. Curly leaves. Fringed lavender and white single flowers.

Volcano. Double red with ruffled gold petal edges. Dark, shiny, ruffled, Supreme foliage.

Voo Doo. Dark, tailored leaves. Dark purple star flowers have darker petal edges.

Vulcan. Single royal purple star flowers with rays of fuchsia pink. Plain foliage.

Westdale Delight. Blooms are semi-double, white with lavender edges. Quilted, serrated foliage.

Westwind's Cherie. Large white fringed semi-double blooms are tinted blue in centers. Medium green, heart-shaped, serrated, tailored foliage.

Westwind's Debbie. Large bright pink fluffy double blooms with darker eyes. Medium green, heart-shaped, tailored foliage.

Westwind's First Snowfall. Medium green, heart-shaped foliage, sometimes ruffled. White frilly single flowers with chartreuse edges in bud.

Westwind's Koko. Quilted leaves. Two-toned cerise double flowers.

Westwind's Linda. Slightly frilled, dark leaves. Frilled light pink double flowers have green edges.

Westwind's Red Eye. Dark green, red-backed, pliable foliage. Bright pink single blooms with deep red eyes.

Westwind's Red Queen. White edged, red single flowers.

Whipped Cream. Black-green, tailored foliage. Full double cream blooms have a bit of pink sprinkled over petals. Small plant.

White Regent. Plain, quilted foliage. Double white flowers with overtones of soft lavender in center.

Who Cares. Medium green, quilted foliage. Medium blue double blooms with darker upper petals.

Wild Wing. Quilted, pointed leaves. White single flower with lavender markings.

Winnie. Dark green, heart-shaped foliage. Wine red blooms are edged in white.

With Pleasure. Heart-shaped, dark, quilted foliage. Rose star blooms with deeper centers and prominent yellow pollen sacs.

Wy'east. Spooned foliage. Double rose-orchid with upper petals of wine red.

Yakima Peach. Fringed, fully double, peach flowers with darker pink and cream petal tips and notched edges. Variegated foliage.

Zee Zee. Frilled, dark foliage and frilled dark blue blooms with white edges.

Zig Zag. Wavy foliage. Blooms are double, purple with gold edges.

Zingo. Very dark leaves. Shaded blue semi-double flowers.

MINIATURES

Baby Dear. Double white, pink-centered flowers.

Baby Pearls. White blooms sometimes are tinted with pink or green. Notched foliage.

Bee Bell. Pink, bell-like blooms are edged in red-pink. Small, tailored foliage.

Blastoff. Dark, tailored foliage. Blue star flowers with pink markings.

Blue and Pink. Double blue or pink blooms occur on one plant.

Chopsticks. Modified girl leaves. Light blue double blooms have wine red petal tips.

Daniel Boone. Tailored leaves. Double white, blue-eyed flowers.

Dolly Dimple. Single blue flowers, girl foliage.

Double Take. Dark strawberry leaves and dark blue double blooms.

Drop Up. Strong, upright, star flowers are colored white to burgundy.

Edith's Toy. Tiny, dark foliage. Pink star flowers.

First Recital. Girl leaves. Lavender blue Geneva blooms.

Gillian. Very dark, quilted leaves. Flowers are powder blue doubles.

Irish Elf Supreme. Scalloped Supreme foliage. White double flowers are marked with green.

Lady Locket Supreme. Tailored foliage. Semi-double white blooms, sometimes with pink flowers, too.

Little Black Sambo. Black-green leaves. Wine red, almost black, blossoms.

Little Crown. Pink and blue star flowers.

Little League. Tiny strawberry leaves. Dark blue double flowers are tinted pink.

Little Maroon. Large, double maroon-purple blooms. Wavy, red-backed foliage.

Little Pink Boy. Large pink double flowers and tailored foliage.

Little Smoky Supreme. Scalloped Supreme foliage. Pearl blue double blooms.

Minnie Ha Ha. Tiny foliage. Shaded mauve and orchid blooms.

Mint Blue. Green-edged double white flowers have blue centers. Tiny foliage.

Pink Up. Double pink blooms. Tiny, dark green, tailored foliage.

Pink Vanilla. Flowers are fringed single pink with white markings.

Rango. Dark quilted leaves and light blue, double flowers.

Rosy Pink. Dark leaves. Rose pink star Geneva blooms.

The Toy. Dark, quilted foliage. Light blue, semi-double flowers with darker markings.

Tiny Blue. Dark leaves and double light blue blooms.

Tiny Pink. Tiny, glossy leaves. Bright pink double blossoms.

Tiny Tina. Flowers are bright pink doubles with deeper centers. Small strawberry foliage.

Tiny Violet. Double violet-blue blooms. Plain green, tiny foliage.

Trinket. Tiny bronze leaves. Magnolia-textured pink single flowers.

Wee Too. Tiny round leaves and double red blooms.

What Not. Serrated leaves. Pink buds and white-edged flowers.

SEMI-MINIATURES

Andy Griffiths. Double burgundy red blooms. Quilted, scalloped and wavy foliage.

Frosty of the Rockies. Medium green, tailored leaves. Semi-double white and lavender flowers.

Hi Friend. Double deep blue with white incurved edges. Notched foliage.

Indian River. Blooms are medium blue doubles. Dark green, quilted foliage.

Jumbo. Slightly wavy leaves and double purple blossoms.

Leslie. Double deep amethyst edge with mauve center. Small, dark, tailored foliage.

Little Deano. Flat, notched, girl leaves. Single white flowers have orchid edges.

Little Miss Texas. Quilted leaves, double white blooms.

Little Red Devil. Almost black leaves with red backs. Red single flowers.

Miss Baton Rouge. Shell pink double blooms.

Miss Willow. Modified girl foliage. Single orchid blooms.

Mountain Sweet Pea. Ruffled, medium green, girl leaves. Single lavender, two-toned, sweet pea-type blooms.

Nancy Ann. Plain green foliage. Light blue single flowers.

Pet. Ruffled leaves. Violet bicolor single blooms.

Pink China. Double brilliant pink flowers. Lightly quilted, slightly glossy foliage.

Pom Pom Delight. Blooms are ruby red doubles. Slightly cupped leaves form a symmetrical wheel of foliage.

Red Beam. Single, intense deep wine red flowers. Heart-shaped, glossy foliage.

Snow Flurry. Tiny leaves. White single blooms have blue eyes.

Susy's Weta. Small foliage and double white blooms.

Sweet Pixie. Delicate pink double flowers. Medium green, tailored foliage.

Vignette. Bubbly girl leaves. Frilled and shaded single blue star flowers.

Window Lace. Wavy, two-toned lilac and mauve double blooms.

Window Wonder. Dark, serrated leaves. Semi-double blue-purple blossoms.

Index

ORGANIZATIONS

If you wish to become more familiar with African violets and other gesneriads, here are the addresses of three societies devoted to the subject. The African Violet Society of America, Inc.—P.O. Box 1326, Knoxville, Tennessee 37901; their journal is *The African Violet Magazine*, published five times a year. The next two societies together publish the bimonthly magazine *Gesneriad-Saintpaulia News*; membership in either society will bring it to you. American Gesneria Society—Worldway Postal Center, Box 91192, Los Angeles, California 90009; Saintpaulia International—P.O. Box 10604, Knoxville, Tennessee 37919.

PHOTOGRAPHERS

HEDRICIS BLESSING: 27. ROBERT COX: 8. RICHARD DAWSON: 48, 51. LOIS B. HAMMOND: 29, 63. ELLS MARUGG: 12 (bottom), 34 (all), 37 (top left). MERRY GARDENS: 52 (right). DON NORMARK: 6, 11 (bottom), 15 (left), 31 (all), 33 (bottom), 38 (bottom), 44, 54 (bottom), 58. ROCHE: 30. ALYSON SMITH: 12 (top), 15 (right), 24 (top), 33 (top), 36 (all), 46 (top), 56 (all), 60, 61 (all), 62 (all). E. FREDERICK SMITH: 45, 55 (top). BETTY STOEHR: 42 (bottom), 47, 49, 52 (left), 55 (bottom). UNITED STATES DEPARTMENT OF AGRICULTURE: 9, 10, 42 (top). DARROW M. WATT: 7, 16, 26, 28, 53. JOYCE R. WILSON: cover, 4, 11 (top), 17 (all), 18 (all), 19, 24 (bottom), 37 (top right, bottom), 38 (top).